SUNFLOWER

New Quilts from an Old Favorite

edited by LINDA BAXTER LASCO

Thank You Sponsors

Clover

JANOME

moda

Located in Paducah, Kentucky, the American Quilter's Society (AQS) is dedicated to promoting the accomplishments of today's quilters. Through its publications and events, AQS strives to honor today's quiltmakers and their work and to inspire future creativity and innovation in quiltmaking.

Executive Book Editor: Andi Milam Reynolds
Senior Editor: Linda Baxter Lasco
Graphic Design: Lynda Smith
Cover Design: Michael Buckingham
Quilt Photography: Charles R. Lynch
In-process photos by quiltmakers unless specified otherwise.

Library of Congress Cataloging-in-Publication Data

Lasco, Linda Baxter.
  Sunflower : new quilts from an old favorite / by Linda Baxter Lasco.
    p. cm.
  ISBN 978-1-57432-658-1
  1. Quilts. 2. Sunflowers in art. 3. Quilting--Competitions--United States. I. American Quilter's Society. II. Title.
  NK9112.L345 2010
  746.46079'73--dc22
                    2010004872

Additional copies of this book may be ordered from the American Quilter's Society, PO Box 3290, Paducah, KY 42002-3290, or online at www.AmericanQuilter.com.

© 2010, American Quilter's Society

Proudly printed and bound in the
United States of America

American Quilter's Society
P. O. Box 3290 • Paducah, KY 42002-3290
www.AmericanQuilter.com

Dedication

This book is dedicated to all those who see a traditional quilt block and can visualize both its link to the past and its bridge to the future.

"Honoring Today's Quilter"

THE NATIONAL QUILT MUSEUM

The National Quilt Museum (NQM) is an exciting place where the public can learn more about quilts, quiltmaking, and quiltmakers, and experience quilts that inspire and delight.

The museum celebrates today's quilts and quiltmakers through exhibits of quilts from the museum's collection and selected temporary exhibits. By providing a variety of workshops and other programs, The National Quilt Museum helps to encourage, inspire, and enhance the development of today's quilter.

Whether presenting new or antique quilts, the museum promotes understanding of and respect for all quilts—contemporary and antique, traditional and innovative, machine made and handmade, utility and art.

Contents

Preface

While preservation of the past is one of a museum's primary functions, its greatest service is performed as it links the past to the present and to the future. With that intention, The National Quilt Museum sponsors an annual contest and exhibit called New Quilts from an Old Favorite (NQOF).

Created to acknowledge our quiltmaking heritage and to recognize innovation, creativity, and excellence, the contest challenges today's quiltmakers to interpret a single traditional quilt block in a new and exciting work of their own design. Each year contestants respond with a myriad of stunning interpretations.

Sunflower: New Quilts from an Old Favorite is a wonderful collection of these interpretations. You'll find a brief description of the 2010 contest, followed by a presentation of the five award winners and 13 finalists and their quilts.

Full-color photographs of the quilts accompany each quiltmaker's comments—comments that provide insight into their widely diverse creative processes. A pattern for the traditional Sunflower block is included to give you a starting point for your own rendition. The winners and finalists' tips, techniques, and patterns offer an artistic framework for your own work.

Our wish is that *Sunflower: New Quilts from an Old Favorite* will further our quiltmaking heritage as new quilts based on the Sunflower block are inspired by the outstanding quilts in this book.

The Contest

The New Quilts from an Old Favorite contest requires that quilts entered be recognizable in some way as a variation of the selected traditional block. The quilts must be no larger than 80" and no smaller than 50" on a side. Each quilt entered must be quilted. Quilts may only be entered by the maker(s) and must have been completed after December 31 two years prior to the entry date.

Quiltmakers are asked to send in two images—one of the full quilt and one detail shot—for jurying. Three jurors view these and consider technique, artistry, and interpretation of the theme block to select 18 finalists from among all the entries. These finalist quilts are then sent to the museum where a panel of three judges carefully evaluates them. The evaluation of the actual quilts focuses on design, innovation, theme, and workmanship. The first- through fifth-place winners are selected and notified.

An exhibit of all the winning and finalist quilts opens at The National Quilt Museum in Paducah each spring, then travels to venues around the country for two years. Thousands of quilt lovers have enjoyed these exhibits nationwide.

A book is produced by the American Quilter's Society featuring full-color photos of the finalist and award-winning quilts, biographical information about each quilter, and tips, techniques, and patterns. The book provides an inside look at how quilts are created and a glimpse into the artistic mindset of today's quilters.

Previous theme blocks have been Double Wedding Ring, Log Cabin, Kaleidoscope, Mariner's Compass, Ohio Star, Pineapple, Storm at Sea, Bear's Paw, Tumbling Blocks, Feathered Star, Monkey Wrench, Seven Sisters, Dresden Plate, Rose of Sharon, Sawtooth, and Burgoyne Surrounded. The Orange Peel block has been selected for the 2011 contest. Baskets and Jacob's Ladder will be the featured blocks for 2012 and 2013.

NQM would like to thank this year's sponsors: Janome America, Inc.; Clover Needlecraft, Inc.; and Moda Fabrics.

The Sunflower Block

Gardening was deemed a suitable pastime for women during the nineteenth century, as was quilting. Both endeavors embodied the idea of moral guidance through a sense of beauty. Women were encouraged to decorate their homes beautifully in order to cultivate an environment in which moral, spiritual, and educational growth of the family could occur.

Parallel to this interest in gardening was an interest in quilting and the language of flowers. Floral motifs have been popular designs since antiquity (witness the leaf forms on Corinthian columns found in ancient Greece), and floral designs in quilts have appeared in the earliest quilts. The language of flowers was a pastime that sparked the publishing of dozens of books one might use for reference as to what flower would convey one's sentiments.[1]

"Sunflower" could mean "adoration"[2]; rose might mean "war," depending on its color. Flowers such as nasturtiums and zinnias were imported in the nineteenth century and opened up new possibilities for gardening with these exotic plants[3] and their ending up in the quilts being produced at this time.

The prosaic sunflower was not a plant a maiden would include in a bouquet. Sturdy, tough, and towering, it did not find its way into quilts until the dominance of the pieced block in the mid-nineteenth century, and then seldom. In fact, the majority of published Sunflower patterns came after the 1920s. In 1929, the sales manager of the Stearns & Foster batting department gave designer Margaret Hays a pencil tracing of a botanical drawing that had appeared in the June 1917 issue of *National Geographic* magazine. She was to use it to rework the Sunflower design from the 1928 batting wrapper. The resultant design proved to be a classic over the years and is often confused with a similar design by Marie Webster.[4]

There are 28 Sunflower block patterns in the *Encyclopedia of Pieced Quilt Patterns*.[5] Sometimes these same blocks went by other names: pattern number 3481 was called Single Sunflower, Blazing Sun, and Blazing Stars in addition to Sunflower.[6] Many appear to the modern eye to be star patterns as no stems or leaves are present. Of approximately 182 Sunflower quilts made before 1950 found in the Quilt Index[7] online, five were the Mountain Mist/ Marie Webster version with the flower blocks arranged along the outer edges so as to encircle a plain inner field; two were *Encyclopedia of Appliqué* pattern 81.4, a *Capper's Weekly* medallion pattern; and all the remaining quilts are block style. The number of petals in these designs varies among eight, nine, 12, 16, 20, and 24. All but a few of these designs date to the 1920s or later.

Was the sunflower not a favored motif in the nineteenth century due to its size and sturdiness? Was it because of its use as feed? Or did its popularity grow after 1920 because of the increase in periodicals and syndicated patterns? We do not know the answers to these questions. We do know that the sunflower, ever turning its face to the sun, has inspired many quiltmakers in the past, as it has inspired the quiltmakers featured in this exhibition.

Judy Schwender
Curator of Collections/Registrar
The National Quilt Museum

1 Susan Curtis, "Blessed Be God for Flowers: Nineteenth-Century Quilt Design" in *A Flowering of Quilts*, Patricia Cox Crews, editor; University of Nebraska Press, 2001, 15.
2 Found at http://aboutflowers.com/flower-a-plant-information-and-photos/meanings-of-flowers.html; accessed 01/07/2010 by the author.
3 Curtis, 12.
4 Merikay Waldvogel, "The Origins of Mountain Mist Patterns" in *Uncoverings 1995*, Volume 16 of the Research Papers of the American Quilt Study Group, Virginia Gunn, editor; AQSG, 1995, 120,122.
5 Barbara Brackman, *Encyclopedia of Pieced Quilt Patterns*; American Quilter's Society, 1993.
6 Ibid., 418.
7 Found at http://www.quiltindex.org; accessed 01/07/2010 by the author.

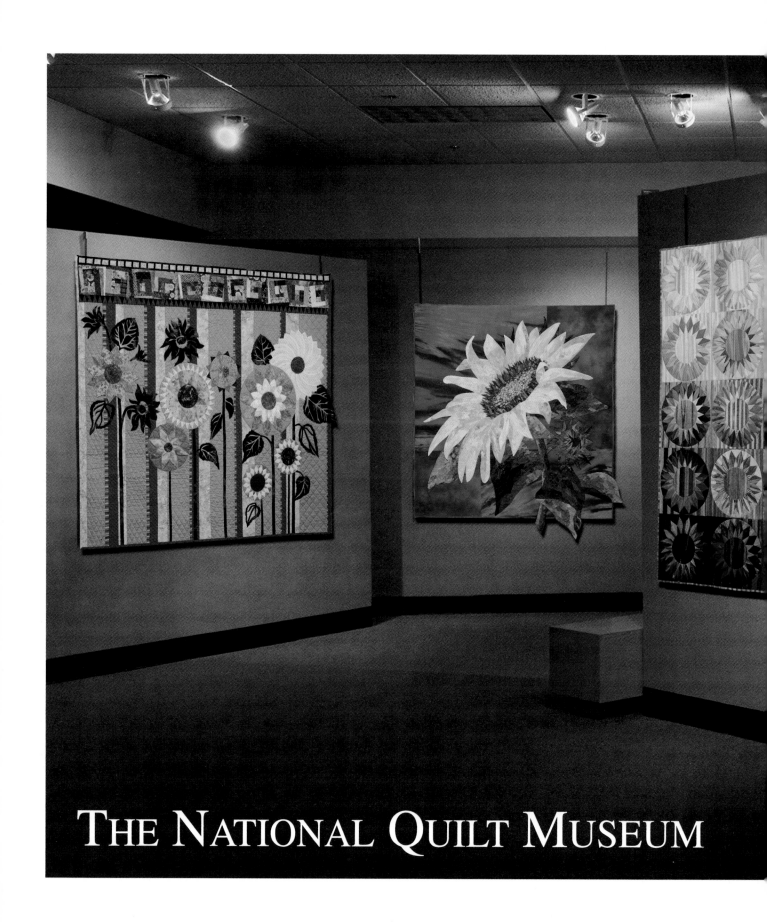

THE NATIONAL QUILT MUSEUM

The National Quilt Museum
215 Jefferson Street • Paducah, Kentucky 42001 • www.quiltmuseum.org • (270) 442-8856

Photo by Thomas Myers

First Place

Claudia Clark Myers
Duluth, Minnesota

Marilyn Badger
St. George, Utah

Photo by Hartley Badger

Meet Claudia

How can it get any better than having an internationally recognized book with your quilt on the cover? Or being treated like royalty at The National Quilt Museum and having a nice, big check put in your hand? Here's what's better—coming around the corner in the museum and seeing OUR quilt, beautifully hung, right there with all the other prize-winning quilts from over the years. Talk about motivation!

I have entered the New Quilts from an Old Favorite contest six times, now—twice with my good friend Marilyn; once with my daughter, Jessica Torvinen; and three times by myself. One of the things I like best about this competition is that it eliminates the blank piece of paper—you already have an assignment, a challenge, a direction in which to start out.

I've always been good at taking an assignment and running with it. I also love working on a deadline. I think about and visualize a project forever and then, as Marilyn can attest, start and finish in a big flurry! More than once, I have Express-mailed entries.

When I first began quilting, I took many quilt classes that used traditional blocks in traditional ways. But before the classes were over, I always had figured out a way to change the setting, skew the block, or use multiple sizes. My favorite instructor asked me once, "Can't you ever do anything the way you're *supposed* to?" Apparently not.

Meet Marilyn

GYPSY CARAVANS was our second collaboration for this contest. The entry deadline of November 1 usually comes when Houston Quilt Festival is going on. Since Claudia and I both work that show, we had to scramble to get our entry finished before we flew off to Houston and then on to the AQS show in Des Moines.

The plan was to have it in my suitcase when leaving for Houston (and it was!) so Claudia could take it home for the finish work and get it entered on time. I would imagine this story sounds very familiar to many quilters who enter competitions!

Design and Inspiration

Claudia
One of my very favorite quotations comes from Scott Adams: "Creativity is allowing yourself to make mistakes. Art is knowing which ones to keep."

Gypsy Caravans 54" x 74"

I always have sunflowers in my garden—whether planted by me or the very helpful red squirrels. In my research, I found many Sunflower blocks, even some that didn't look remotely like a sunflower. I chose one and added the encircling ring seen in some of the other variations. That was design change #1. There were many more to follow.

Fig. 1

I always go through this with every quilt. I call it "Quilt Agony." While it is happening, I am ornery, short-tempered, and generally no fun to live with. My studio is a disaster with paper foundations and little fabric samples all over. I am fortunate to have a small group of friends and relatives I trust to make suggestions. I may not always take them, but I do listen. I also e-mail pictures to Marilyn as the quilt takes shape so she can see the progress and jump in with any ideas.

All of the blocks I saw were meant to be pieced. I redrafted mine to be mostly machine appliquéd—change #2 (fig. 1). I like blocks or elements of differing sizes, so I took my design to the copy shop and had four different-sized flowers printed—change #3.

Along the way, the configuration changed several times and the background changed three times, including ditching the one that I had taken all the flower colors from. It wound up being the binding fabric. What a come-down (figs. 2–3)!

Fig. 2

Fig. 3

As the quilt evolved and the pieces got shoved around on the wall, the memory of a photograph I had taken one summer at The House on the Rock in Wisconsin came rushing into my mind (fig. 4). At that point, the name changed to GYPSY CARAVANS.

One of the last design decisions came the night before the finished quilt top got sent to Marilyn for quilting. I was still trying to get that wonderful fabric that had started out as the background into the quilt and had added side borders of it (fig. 5).

Just before I put it into the shipping box, I whacked them off! Sometimes design changes can be thoughtful, planned-out, carefully selected decisions and sometimes they come right out of the blue and you *know* they are right!

Marilyn

Since my style of quilting is very dense, it was necessary to come up with designs to quilt in all the petals of the sunflowers (or spokes of the wheels if you're thinking Gypsy wagons, which is the way I was looking at it). Since the fabrics were mostly prints and very colorful, I didn't think the quilting would really show up other than in perfect lighting. Even so, it still needed dense quilting in order to avoid distortion. I sketched one half of a wheel and

Fig. 5

Fig. 4

doodled around with different ways to fill the spaces, then chose the ones that were best suited for the design.

At the mid-point of quilting the entire row of spokes in one of the large wheels I had to roll the quilt to work on the bottom half of the wheel. It just so happened that the spool of thread I was using ran out at this time so this was where I decided to end my evening of quilting. The next day I threaded on a new spool and finished the bottom half. You guessed it, the thread was a different shade. Because of the quilting density, it took three days to rip out stitches in an area that originally took only a couple of hours to complete.

Testing and distributing quilting designs

The navy background areas were saved for last. I knew I wanted to pull the wheel designs out and quilt them in gold thread. I chose Superior Brytes™ thread because it is a heavier thread (30 wt.) and really shows up well.

New Quilts from an Old Favorite is really a fun contest. I'm pleased to have been able to participate with Claudia. Her designs are always eye-catching and fun to work on. It is a thrill to see our work hanging among all the other finalists' quilts in the exhibit at the museum during the AQS show in Paducah. Of course, being in the book is an added bonus. It makes those deadlines easy to handle and ripping sessions well worth the effort!

Second Place

Geri Parker
Coupeville, Washington

Photo by Bruce C. McNeil

Kathy McNeil
Marysville, Washington

Meet Geri and Kathy

Kathy and I have been collaborating on one quilt a year for about four years. She considers me a traditional quilter while she does appliqué pictorial quilts. When she asked me to partner with her in making a quilt, I was surprised, scared, and elated as her competition quilts have won many awards. My quilting career started about 30 years ago, making quilts for family and charity. Babies/children don't expect points to meet. Although I usually don't make quilts from a pattern, most of my quilts are more traditional.

Kathy starts by designing our quilts. Although she has a visual image of where she wants to go with a project, rarely does it end up looking like the first sketch.

The approach is to put something down and then reevaluate and start over if it doesn't go where we thought or hoped it would. This approach fascinates me and gives us great freedom to be creative. We take it layer by layer, designing from the center out.

Since I live on an island and Kathy is in town, about one and a half hours apart, our quilt work consists of lots of e-mails, phone calls, and ferry rides to discuss, view, or work together. We are both very blessed in having husbands who encourage and appreciate our quilting.

We love continuing the long tradition of quilting with a dear friend. It is a crazy adventure every time. What a treat!

Our Sunflower Quilt

We have wanted to try a challenge quilt for The National Quilt Museum for some time. Being innovative with a sunflower seemed especially challenging. We had fun trying to capture the *essence* of a sunflower, with its radiance and constant movement at the slightest breeze. There were many trips to the fabric stores, trying to find prints that would capture and express a sunflower without using the expected colors. When you design layer by layer as we do, frequent gut-wrenching trips are required to get more, please, please, of the fabrics that actually did work.

The 8" "pot holders," our unique Sunflower blocks, were my first challenge. Paper piecing made this much easier. When these were done, Kathy decided we needed to add the black and white saw-blade outside radial edge for a more dramatic look. Sunflowers are not shy. The black petals were machine embroidered by Kathy with gold metallic thread. Twenty-four radiant sun points extend from the sunflower's center machine-appliquéd silhouette design. Under each is a shadow of light, created by a slightly larger, lighter shape. Repeating the radial black and white points and the sunflower silhouette shapes in the corners completed the design.

Sun Flower Duet 69½" x 66½"

Our Sunflower Block

Our Sunflower block is 6½" in diameter (fig. 1). We began with the traditional eight-pointed Sunflower Star block. The outside edge was cut as a circle, ½" wider than the points. The center was sewn to netting then turned (fig. 2). Appliquéd over the center of the star is a small circle of black-and-white novelty print.

The petals were machine appliquéd using Ultrasuede® Light fabric. Freezer paper was used as template material to keep the petal size consistent. Ultrasuede has the wonderful advantage of not fraying. Black and white paper-pieced spinners were added around the circumference of the gold circle (fig. 3).

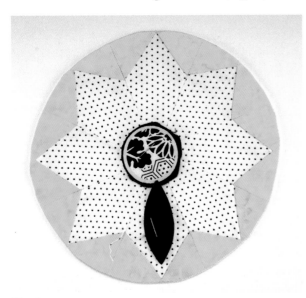

Fig. 1

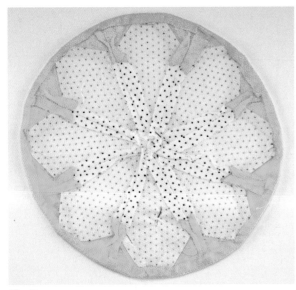

Fig. 2

Capitulum—sunflower head

Freeform fun and breezy Ultrasuede shapes were machine appliquéd in the center with gold metallic thread, placing three small sunflower designs in the middle (fig. 4). Purple ombre fabric was cut and pieced specifically to allow light to emanate from the center. These shapes were repeated on the outside corners for unity.

Black cording separates the flower head from the focal sunflower blocks. Gold metallic embroidery stitches completed the center.

Double piping was repeated around the final outer black circle. Black gave a dynamic look to the center medallion of our design.

Twenty-four sun rays were placed behind and between each focal Sunflower block. Sunflowers are all about catching sun rays. They turn on the stalk so that they are always facing the sun. This fun fact became a design element in our quilt. A larger ray was needed between the Sunflower blocks so that it would touch the capitulum (head) of the sunflower design. To simulate a brighter light effect, light lavender fabric star rays were placed under the "pillow-

Fig. 3

cased" sun rays. The ends were left to curl up much like sunflower petals. Machine embroidery was added along each edge to create a glow.

Outer scallops

We added 14 outer scallops using half of a 10" circle to create movement around the inside medallion (fig. 5). They are slightly larger in scale than the 6" focal Sunflower blocks. The saw-blade edge was paper pieced for preci-

sion. The trapuntoed ghost image sunflower was machine embroidered in contrasting thread.

Kathy's home machine quilting finished this exuberant creation. The quilt was squared and trimmed. The double curved border was measured to a $1/16$" for a perfect mitered corner. Made with the pillow slip technique, the front of the border was sewn to the quilt as you would a binding and the back turned under ½" and hand sewn to the back of the quilt as per normal.

Fig. 4

Fig. 5

Sharon V. Rotz

Mosinee, Wisconsin

Photo by Sharon V. Rotz

Meet Sharon

It's color. It's pattern. It's touching and feeling. It's the excitement of combining fabrics in a new way.

It's measuring. It's precision of cutting. It's the power of machine stitching across the surface uniting these fragments of fabric into a whole.

It's creativity. It's a sense of accomplishment. It's the link to generations of women. These are the things that draw me to quilting.

Quilting entered my life after I had finished college (in the field of home economics, no less), married, and had children. Having many ideas of how sewing should be done, I slid into quilting sideways, questioning my quilting teachers at every turn. I was a true teacher's nightmare.

Despite myself, I did learn traditional quilting methods, but always lurking just under the traditional surface was a rebellious side waiting to be let loose. The more confident I became in my new quilting world, the more I opened up to my creative side. This was, and still is, an ongoing process, giving myself permission to make quilts simply for the joy of creating. LEANING ON THE FENCE is an example of my struggle as I tiptoe on the fence between traditional quilter and artist.

My enthusiasm for touching and working with fabrics has spread out to encouraging others, teaching, planning my own projects, and designing and selling my own patterns. With the encouragement of others, I proposed an idea for a quilting book. This led to the rewarding opportunity of sharing my love of fabric even more through the privilege of writing three quilting books.

My artistic side pulled me into a world of ever new experiments with color and pattern. How could I change and improve what I had done before? I feel a great sense of urgency in my work. Again, my enthusiasm for working with fabrics pushes me to share my work. I enjoy creating my own artworks, entering art shows, and exhibiting my art quilts in gallery settings in an attempt to open others to the beauty of quilting.

Inspiration and Design

I was inspired by a piece of fabric that didn't even make it into the quilt. How does that work? It works when you keep your options open. I recently fell in love with an a graphic print with rings of rust, gold, blue, and olive. Immediately, I cut it up to use with an olive linen for the background of a quilt. This fabulous fabric didn't even have time to "season" in my stash.

In an attempt to add elements to my basic idea, sunflowers began to dominate my thoughts. I started to construct several different styles and sizes, but they were not working on my framed

Leaning on the Fence 62" x 56"

Fig. 2

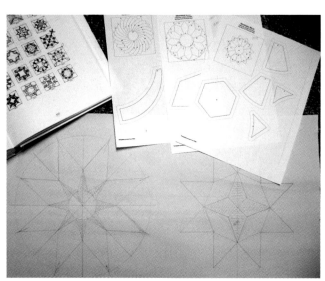
Fig. 1

medallion-style background. My sunflowers couldn't grow around in a circle but needed to reach for the sky. They needed a linear background and the background made of my inspirational fabric was abandoned.

I thought of making a fence that changed across the width of the quilt, giving a feeling of perspective. While the olives, yellows, golds, and rust worked well together, they were in need of a contrasting color to set them off. After digging through my stash and trying different fabrics, a scrap of turquoise became the deal breaker (fig. 1). Off I went to the quilt shop to find a quantity of turquoise fabric.

Now I was happy with the background for my sunflowers. A recently purchased dark batik provided the leaves and stems. (See what happens when you are standing in the cutting line at the quilt shop and the person in front of you has the perfect fabric?) I picked actual sunflower leaves for the leaf patterns.

Although my sunflowers refused to be trapped by borders, a single border on the top of the quilt felt right. My favorite Log Cabin "freedom blocks" were a whimsical solution marrying the fabrics of the quilt into a colorful display across the top. Tilting and turning, they provided relief from the regimented straight lines of the body of the quilt.

Techniques

Each new quilt builds upon the techniques explored, practiced, or perfected in past quilts. I can see this continually happening in my quilting. In LEANING ON THE FENCE, my sunflowers became a sampler quilt of piecing options. After researching Sunflower blocks (fig. 2), I started by hand drafting some of them. I soon switched over to the computer and my Electric Quilt® software for quicker results. I used Debra Wagner's Sunflower block and her Striplate Piecing method, combining strip-piecing and templates. Paper piecing worked well for another block. Some sunflowers were easy to machine piece, while others seemed to be made for relaxing hand piecing.

Making Freedom Log Cabin Blocks

After the diversity of methods used for the sunflowers, I came back to my favorite Freedom Log Cabin blocks for the top border. Using scrap strips for these blocks makes it easy to add abundant color and pattern.

The scale of strip width to the total block size is important. On smaller blocks, strips should range from 1¼" to 2¾" wide. A wide strip can easily be trimmed before adding the next log. The more variety you have in the widths, the more interest there will be in the blocks.

Start with a center square or rectangle, cutting any size that is in scale with the size of the finished block (for example, a 2" center for a 6" finished block). Add strips around the center, varying the color and fabric patterns. You are not looking for a light and dark side in the block but a random happening of fabrics (fig. 3).

Continue adding strips until the block is 1" to 1½" larger than the desired unfinished block size. Your block may no longer be square and the center may no longer be exactly in the middle. The varying widths of strips will give your blocks wonderful attitude.

Mark a square ruler the unfinished block size and place it over the block, tilting it as much as possible. Trim two sides. Turn the block, reposition the ruler, and trim the remaining two sides. Place all the blocks trimmed with the ruler tilted to the right (fig. 4) in one pile and an equal number of blocks trimmed with the ruler tilted to the left (fig. 5) in another pile. Alternate the blocks when placing them in your quilt.

Fig. 3

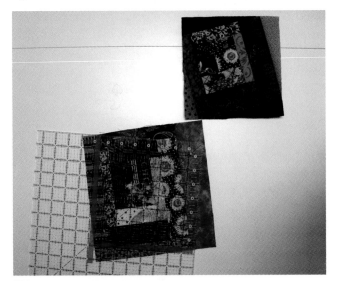

Fig. 4

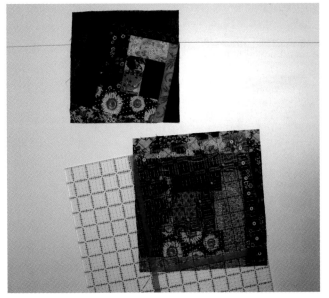

Fig. 5

Fourth Place

Ronna Erickson
Amherst, Massachusetts

Photo by Neal Erickson

Ann Feitelson
Montague, Massachusetts

The Collaboration

Ann has always been impressed with Ronna's unflappability in the face of technical challenges. Ronna remains intrigued by Ann's spectacular use of punchy color and her drive to complete quilts for competitions. Long-time members of a monthly Round Robin, they have worked together on many group projects, but this is their first true collaboration. This quilt was begun just after Labor Day, when sunflowers in Massachusetts gardens were at their peak, and finished in two months.

Meet the Quilters

Ann
My quilts are about color more than anything else. I am passionately attracted to rich colors and fascinated by the way they shift depending on how they are juxtaposed. My inspiration is nature. Once a landscape painter (I have masters degrees in painting and art history), I am beguiled by landscape. On my regular bike rides along the Connecticut River, I savor the views of trees against sky, water, and hills; the varied textures of leaves, weeds, and grasses; the different colorations of weather and season. This spring, knowing of the contest, I planted some sunflower seeds, imagining that the flowers would inspire me when they bloomed, and they did.

Ronna
My interests have always been quite varied and split equally between art and science. Leonardo Da Vinci was my childhood hero. As a child, I spent countless hours studying nature and drawing what I observed. I often created all sorts of things from various materials, especially from cloth and fibers. I also enjoyed assembling and disassembling very small mechanical items. As I grew older, the lure of textiles led to a BFA from Syracuse University in surface pattern design.

After freelancing in the industry, science again called to me and I received a degree in astrophysics. Currently, I build instrumentation for radio astronomy, where both my art and science skills are used in my daily work.

I still work in many areas of textile arts and what I learn from one I apply to the others. I tend to be process oriented and enjoy just working on something with my hands and figuring out how to do it. I have amassed a wide variety of UFOs and enjoy working on all of them, whether they ever get completed or not!

Rising and Radiant 60½" x 60½"

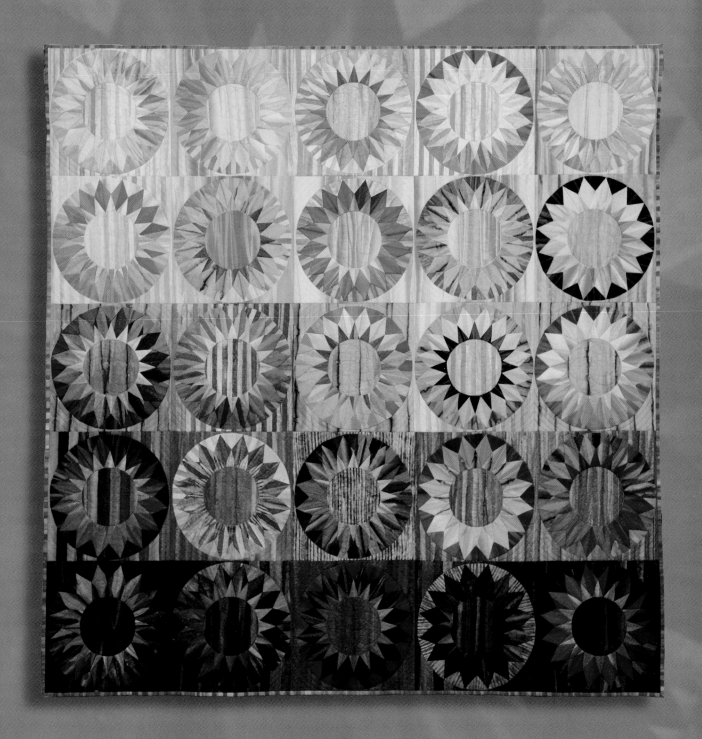

Inspiration and Design

Ann

I began by piecing the blocks. Each one was an experiment in combining and sequencing color. I imagined the variety of colors representing sunflowers as they appear in different kinds of light—from high noon to diffuse haze to deep shadow. I also thought of the sunflower in all stages of its life cycle—the tender bud, the vibrant flower, the dark husk—and the colors are also meant to represent those phases of maturity.

The sunflower came to symbolize a life force, pure botanical and floral energy. The sunflower, the sun, the circle: all have a kind of primal potency, and these blocks, with their three rings of shifting, circulating color came excitingly close to expressing that.

The pieced circles are about the experience of looking at sunflowers (or even the sun), being dazzled by bright, radiating orbs in a bright space.

Stripes are another primal force, both visual and botanical. Aligned vertically, they represent stems, upward growth, movement towards the sun. Cut to align with the axes of the abstract petals, they radiate.

Ronna

When I saw Ann's first radiating rings on striped backgrounds, I loved the idea of creating a vibrant garden of these spectacular flowers and eagerly accepted her invitation to collaborate on the project. Despite a scientific background in analytical techniques, I am intuitive in my placement of color. I also view the quilt as a three-dimensional (albeit very thin!) object. The placement of fabrics of differing values help give the illusion of depth. Careful placement of color will lead the eye around the quilt, constantly intriguing the viewer and pulling attention from one area to another.

As more rings were pieced, we put them on different backgrounds, and I reacted to the flow from one area of the quilt to another. We worked together to remove all impediments to the flow of color. The brilliance and clarity of the colors in this quilt give the flowers a scintillating effect, which expresses the idea of sunshine and heat—the essence of sunflower.

Technique

Ronna

After the rings were pieced, it was necessary to true them up to size and roundness. With a precision compass, two circles were drawn on a muslin ironing board cover using the inner raw edge radius and the outer raw-edge radius measurements (fig. 1).

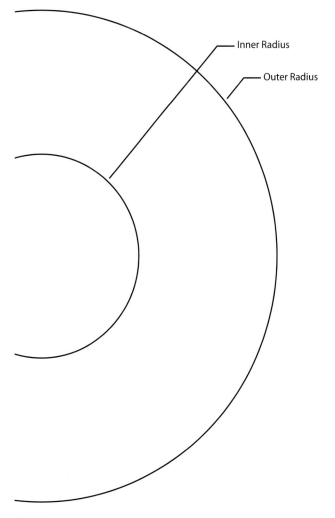

Inner Radius

Outer Radius

Fig. 1

Then, using my well-honed technique of "persuasive pressing," I convinced the rings to match the drawn lines and so enforce the roundness of the rings. Persuasive pressing is done using a dry iron, pins, and a spray bottle of water. It is a technique used in making shaped couture clothing and it works very well with cotton used in quilting, allowing one to compensate for the inaccuracies that occur when piecing a complicated block.

Each ring was placed wrong-side up, moistened with a fine mist, and massaged until it reached the drawn lines (fig. 2). Then it was pinned to the ironing board with the pins running horizontally under the ironing board cover (figs. 3–4). (I use metal or glass-head pins that will not melt if ironed.)

Fig. 2

After the rings are pinned and the seam allowances arranged, a dry iron is used to steam-set them (fig 5). Allow them to cool before unpinning. Finally, press from the right side.

Fig. 3

After we trued the blocks, we carefully drafted and cut donut-shaped freezer-paper templates. We ironed them to the wrong side of the blocks, pressed the seam allowances over the edges of the freezer paper, and machine basted the seam allowances in place.

We used polyester monofilament thread to machine appliqué the rings so we could cross the wide variety of colors without changing threads or taking the focus away from the rings.

Fig. 4

Quilting

The quilt-as-you-go technique, which neither of us had ever attempted before, allowed for detailed quilting of eight small circles in the center of individual blocks without having to maneuver a big bulky quilt. Final echo curved quilting was done after the entire quilt was assembled.

Fig. 5

Fifth Place

Helena Scheffer
Montreal, Quebec, Canada

Photo by David Hudson

Marion Perrault
Montreal, Quebec, Canada

Meet the Quilters

Marion

Although there were no quilters in my immediate family, I had always done sewing, crafts, and doll making, so I had a lot of fabric that I thought I could get rid of by making a quilt. No classes were available here in the '70s, so I bought a *McCall's* magazine with a page of instructions and made a Jacob's Ladder quilt using cardboard templates.

Originally I had wanted to study at the Ontario College of Art, but decided that nursing might be a more practical choice. I ended up working out of Montreal as a flight attendant, where I met my husband. At that time, all flight attendants had to be nurses. We settled in the Montreal suburb of Beaconsfield and had three children, all of whom now have vast collections of my work decorating their walls.

A friend of mine introduced me to the Vermont Quilt Festival, which was an eye-opening experience. Then I went to Quilt National in 1979 where I saw how far the "craft" of quilting had evolved. I began to take all manner of classes and entered competitions as often as possible. I find that having my work judged by a variety of people who don't know me or my work to be very interesting and instructional.

In the beginning, I made the usual traditional quilts, but I soon stopped using patterns and started playing with fabric, following the "cut it out and put it on a design wall to see how it looks" school of quilting. I especially enjoy the ruler-free style of cutting. I rarely make bed quilts and prefer to just have fun without having to think about the final size of the quilt, what color it should be, or where it will go.

Helena

My first contact with quilting was a bus trip to the Vermont Quilt Festival 22 years ago. I had seen a poster at our local quilt shop, booked a ticket, and hopped onto the bus, not knowing a soul or a thing about quilting. I was completely dazzled by the fabulous quilts and bitten by the quilting bug. I never expected that quilting would change my life as much as it has. Amish quilts were my first love. I was mesmerized by the interplay of their strong, saturated colors. I later began to experiment with my own designs and play with fabric painting and dyeing.

I am a native Montrealer, where I live with my husband and three dogs. I consider myself truly fortunate to have not only a supportive family and a fulfilling career as a French-to-English translator, but also a consuming passion for quilting. My two daughters are my biggest fans and proudly display some of my favorite quilts in their apartments. I also love to cook and my cookbook collection is rivaled only by my shelves of quilt books.

Sunflower Sutra 56" x 58"

My latest venture is Galerie Ouest (www.galerieouest.ca), an art gallery operated as a no-commission rental space. It has exhibited work by hundreds of artists and I have curated a few themed shows myself. The latest was a fundraiser that collected $3,200 for local animal shelters.

Marion and I began collaborating five years ago. Quilting, like translation, is often an introspective solo process, so it is great fun to work with a partner. SUNFLOWER SUTRA is our fifth joint project. We worked on this quilt all summer, all day, almost every day (fig. 1). We are really pleased with the end result and I think there may be other flowers in our future.

Helena on Inspiration and Design

This contest theme was a real challenge for us both. Neither of us are "flower people." I have nary a floral print in my extensive collection, so we were really starting with a blank slate when it came to designing a floral quilt.

We began by looking carefully at sunflowers: buying them at the market, perusing books at the library, and researching them online. Ask us anything about sunflowers! We can now tell you more about them than you would ever need to know. We carefully studied real sunflowers to try to understand how the light and dark areas created the bends and folds. We drew some sketches and started to work (fig. 2).

Helena on Technique

The center of the flower is particularly interesting, since the seeds are arranged in a spiral pattern known as the Fibonacci sequence, first described by the twelfth-century Italian mathematician of that name. We used a technique

Fig. 1

Fig. 2

on the center that I first developed in a Klimt-inspired quilt of my dog Daisy, fusing layers of ovals onto a background fabric.

Each petal is created individually, starting with a paper pattern. Hundreds of pieces of fabric, many of them artist-dyed, were placed on a flannel foundation, then heavily quilted through a tulle overlay. The veins of the petals and leaves were added with heavier thread. We straight stitched and painted the edges to seal them (fig. 3).

We redid many of the petals several times to achieve the dimensional look we were trying for. The leaves, stem, and bud were created the same way. The "frill" around the center is made of individual pieces of fabric backed by fusible web that gives them body. They are not ironed down and are attached only at the base. They have taken on a life of their own over time, twisting into interesting shapes.

I dyed the fabric for the background and then free-motion machine quilted it like a whole-cloth quilt before the flower was applied. Unfortunately, my favorite parts of the quilting were covered by the petals. Wouldn't you know it!

Once all of the elements were created, we pinned them to the background and quilted them down. French knots were added last for additional texture. After it was all finished, Marion woke up at 5 o'clock one morning with a vision of another leaf on the left side. OK, so the quilt was not quite complete yet! She unpicked all the quilting, we created another leaf, and added it on—a great decision since it adds the necessary balance to the piece. Sometimes you get your best ideas in the middle of the night!

Fig. 3

Finalist

Kathryn Botsford

Campbell River, British Columbia, Canada

Photo by Anthony Pinder

Meet Kathryn

FOLLOW THE SUN (ON ROUTE 66) is the first quilt I made in my new studio, which is part of the new addition on our house. I started quilting eight years ago, but worked out of my study and the kitchen. The house started to fill up with plastic bins of fabric, threads, yarn, notions, etc. I love my new studio, as do our cats; they seem to think we built it for them. My husband and I are both animal lovers—we have three cats and two dogs. They came from the local SPCA.

I come from a family of sewers, but I am the first quilter in my family. I like to enter shows, challenges, and contests because they motivate me to explore different areas of quilting. My quilt METROPOLIS IN BLOOM was one of the finalists in the Rose of Sharon: New Quilts from an Old Favorite 2007 contest. The creative journey of a quilt artist is wonderful!

In my professional life, I am in my thirty-third year of teaching public school. I truly enjoy teaching; being surrounded by the joyful energy of young children and their love of learning continues to be a gift.

Inspiration and Design

I love sunflowers. My mother was an incredible gardener and year after year we would have a row of stately sunflowers along our vegetable garden. Immature sunflowers face east every morning waiting for the sun to rise and turn to track the sun throughout the day before returning to face the east again at night. The word for sunflower in French is *tournesol*, which literally means turn with the sun. When sunflowers are mature they permanently face east, perhaps as a defense to protect the seeds from the scalding sun on hot days.

I knew I wanted to make a quilt for this year's contest. I have been collecting fabric for a couple of years to make a sunflower quilt, but I changed directions when I saw the Alexander Henry Route 66 fabric collection.

During my teenage years in the Detroit area in the 1960s, I had the dream of following the sun on Route 66 to sit beneath the palm trees of California's sun-drenched Pacific coastline. This highway is not only a physical route, but also a state of mind. Its image was built on myth, but to me it represented freedom, romance, and adventure.

The 2,400 mile east-west highway from Chicago to Los Angeles was designated as Route 66 in 1926. It no longer appears on maps but 85 percent is still easily drivable. Route 66 is now more about memories; it is a road that refuses to die.

I wanted to create a quilt that was folksy and bright with its focus on the sunflowers, while representing the Route 66 of yesterday and today. I wanted the nostalgia of this highway to

Follow the Sun (on Route 66)

53½" x 52½"

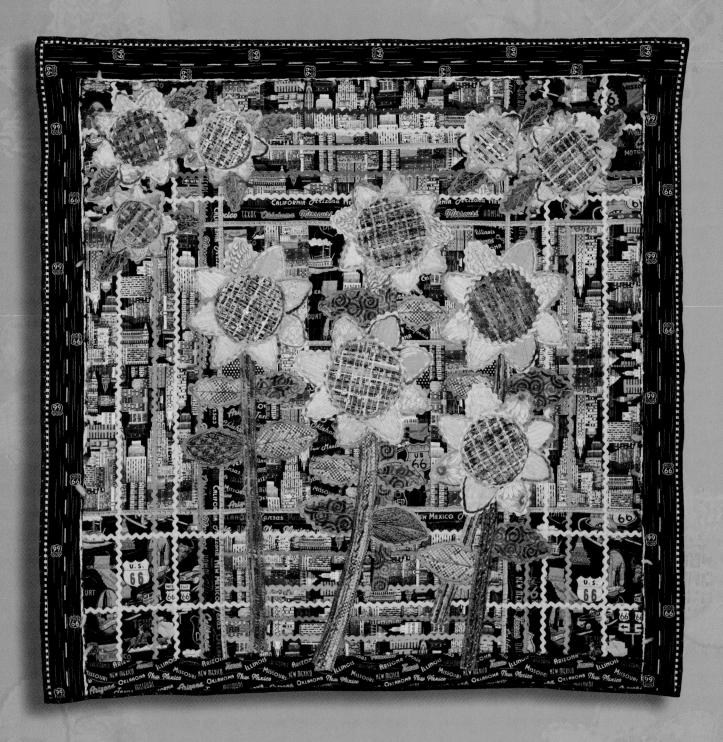

be visible, but I also wanted it to be a bit rough and unkempt (as many parts of Route 66 are today) bathed in larger-than-life sunflowers.

I came up with my unconventional construction process through trial and error to create the results I wanted. As I sat and looked at the completed quilt I had a sense of yesterday and today, and felt peace in the journey I had traveled from immaturity to maturity while looking forward to the future.

Background

This quilt background was constructed in layers and pieces, not unlike the construction of Route 66. The quilt background represents a mature Route 66. The early days of it are veiled with sections of the past peeking through, and mature sunflowers take their place over the past dreams and journeys. The quilt border only has the Route 66 fabric strips on three sides to represent the broken and disconnected areas of it today.

The background is made with sixteen 12½" (unfinished) blocks. I joined them in five sections. The sections and the border strips were sandwiched to Hobbs Thermore® batting and quilted separately. Additional fabric strips were added to the center section prior to quilting.

Trim (ribbon and rickrack) was pinned to the background on the design wall (fig. 1), and after several days of pinning and re-pinning,

Fig. 1

I had the combination that worked for me. I used rickrack as the main trim because of its nostalgic value and current revival, as with the current revival of Route 66 (fig. 2).

I added the quilted borders, then sandwiched the top with another layer of batting and backing and added more quilting. Black and white yarn was sewn along the highway border to create an unkempt look along Route 66. The broken and uneven stitching was done on the road to reflect the current condition of the highway.

Sunflower

The rich and textured center was created to represent the 1,000–2,000 tiny flowers that are joined at the base of the sunflower's head; eventually each flower will produce a seed. I traced a circle on a piece of batting. I layered it with a square of fabric and sewed around the drawn line from both sides (fig. 3). Then I created a grid over the circle with pieces of different novelty yarns, sewn in place and trimmed at the edge of the circle (fig. 4).

I cut a piece of rickrack a little larger than the circumference of the circle, then pinned and stitched it in place (fig. 5). I couched novelty yarn over the rickrack and trimmed the excess batting and fabric just under the edge of the rickrack (fig. 6). I steam pressed with a protective cloth.

The petals, leaves, and stem were done in a similar fashion (fig. 7). Then the center and petals were joined to form the sunflower head (fig. 8).

I pinned the heads, stems, and leaves to the quilted background on the design wall (fig. 9). I arranged and rearranged them over a couple days until I got the look I liked. I photographed them before I took them off the quilt. I joined the leaves and stems in the same way I made the sunflower head. The completed sunflowers were repositioned on the quilt, sewn in place, and steam pressed as before.

Fig. 2

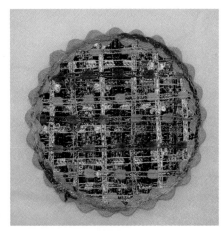

Fig. 6

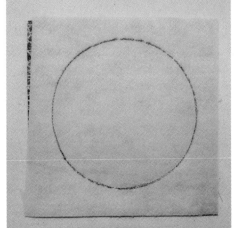

Fig. 3

Fig. 7

Fig. 4

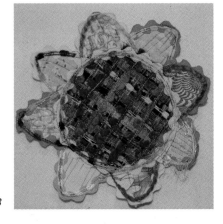

Fig. 8

Fig. 5

Fig. 9

Finalists

Jill Bryant
Chesterfield, Missouri

Nancy S. Brown
Oakland, California

Photo by Jill Bryant

Photo by Laurel Putnam

Meet the Quilters

Jill

Like most of you reading these words, I have been sewing and trying out multiple needle crafts all my life. Once I discovered quilting, all other crafts went by the wayside. Cross stitch? Hours spent over a teensy 15" x 15" project when I could quilt a 50" x 50" project in the same time? Nope. Crewel? Crochet? Knitting? Nope again, it's *all* about quilting.

I love to create and rarely follow a published pattern, but I discovered that sometimes taking a pattern idea and making it my own can cause "creative challenges of design or construction."

Self-taught with help from my guild quilter buddies, I thought I didn't need instructions. So when I first saw foundation piecing, I was excited to try it. But did I read the part about dialing down the stitch length to perforate the paper, thus making removal easier? Nope. Since then, if I follow another quilter's published design, *I read all the instructions*, but I still love the challenge of creating my own way. Thank you, Nancy, for another wonderful design to put together and quilt! I love our sunflowers.

Nancy

I have been quilting for 20 years. I learned to appliqué and quilt from my mother. I love hand appliqué and I love animals. My quilts almost always combine these two loves. I teach a lot of classes in appliqué and designing animal quilts at various shops, guilds, and confer-

ences, but I always find time to work on my own quilts, too. I think my continuing students enjoy seeing and learn a lot by watching my entire process from drawing the design to quilting the quilt.

Even though this is only the second quilt I have made that incorporates flowers, I really love do love them. I inherited this love of flowers from my father. When I was a child I would help him in the garden and we would go to flower shows together. Two of his favorite flowers were roses and sweet peas. Today I have several rose bushes and I plant sweet peas every year in his memory.

Nancy on Inspiration and Design

When Jill and I decided to make this quilt, the first thing I thought was that we shouldn't take the block literally but rather take the shapes of the sunflower as a launching pad and create a totally new design with them—preferably something involving animals. After all, I said, everyone will be doing sunflowers.

I had vague visions of the petals forming the mane of a lion or perhaps the wings or feathers on colorful fantasy birds. Jill kept sending sketches of flower designs, but I kept saying, "No sunflowers!" She did try to draw other designs and my favorite was a recurring creature that we couldn't agree was a peacock or a turkey (figs. 1–2, page 38).

Crowing for Sunflowers 55" x 55"

Fig. 1

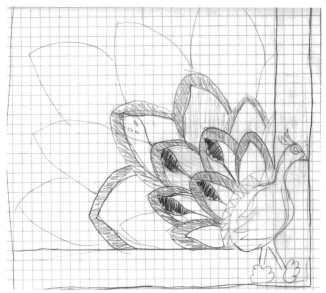

Fig. 2

Fig. 3

When I finally sat down to sketch my lions and fantasy birds, the designs just didn't work. Just for fun, I thought I'd try a sunflower, and the design came rather quickly after that. We have crows in our neighborhood and I thought their black feathers and dramatic shape would be a nice contrast to the rest of the quilt. I used some of Jill's sunflower ideas (fig. 3) and even turned her turkey/peacock/dahlia into one of the sunflowers (fig. 4).

This is the second time that Jill and I have made a quilt together and I think the second time was easier. It helped that my appliqué sections and Jill's piecing sections were independent of each other so we didn't have to keep shipping things back and forth or wait for one to finish one part to begin the next.

The design was more sketchy than the last time and there was room for individual interpretation. Working as a team was an enjoyable experience and provided for a lot of feedback. It was also highly motivating for getting things done. (We are equal opportunity naggers.) I have a feeling that this won't be our last quilt together.

Jill on Technique

When Nancy sent me the final design, I first drew a full-sized, on-point square so I could draw out the flowers that would then become my patterns. I wanted to add something to the center and tried ruching (fig. 5), but sorry, it was too hard to get flat, so I opted for half circles. I placed embroidery floss around the petals to see the effect and it was working for me (fig. 6).

I used the full-size drawing to trace on freezer paper, machine appliquéing the flower petals and centers with a blind hem stitch. I fused the lightest weight Pellon® interfacing to the lighter yellows to eliminate shadowing. I followed the same method for the other yellow petals.

Nancy on Technique

I appliquéd the crows by hand. I prefer needle-turn hand appliqué. I enjoy the process and the results. I also prefer to appliqué the entire crow before appliquéing it to a background (as opposed to appliquéing one piece at a time to the background).

If you want your crow (page 41) to have some dimension you have to understand that when light hits the black feathers areas of light and shadow are created. For the wing (piece #5) to come forward a little, choose a black print that reads lighter than the one that you choose for the body (#1). To make the other wing (#3) recede a little, choose a solid black. Fabric with lines will suggest tail feathers (#2 and #4). I used prints with a lot of white in them for #4. The beak (#6) is a dark grey and just for fun I used a black/grey stripe for the feet (#7).

Jill on Quilting

Nancy was to send me her blocks so I would have time to assemble the top and quilt it. Assembly took longer than expected and by the time I began quilting, I only had six weeks until the deadline. Panic didn't set in until about week four when the unfinished area was still *huge*. (Please, don't tell Nancy.) I was working 50 hours a week on my job, quilting 10–12 hours on Saturday and Sunday, and I was running out of time. (I didn't *dare* let on to Nancy.)

I love the quilt in spite of the panic and love working with Nancy, but truth be told, I now know I don't quilt as fast as I thought! Nancy? I need two months to quilt the next one.

Fig. 4

Fig. 5

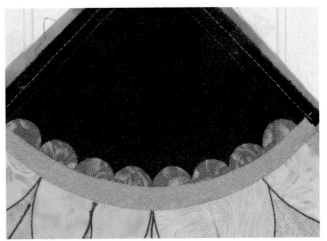

Fig. 6

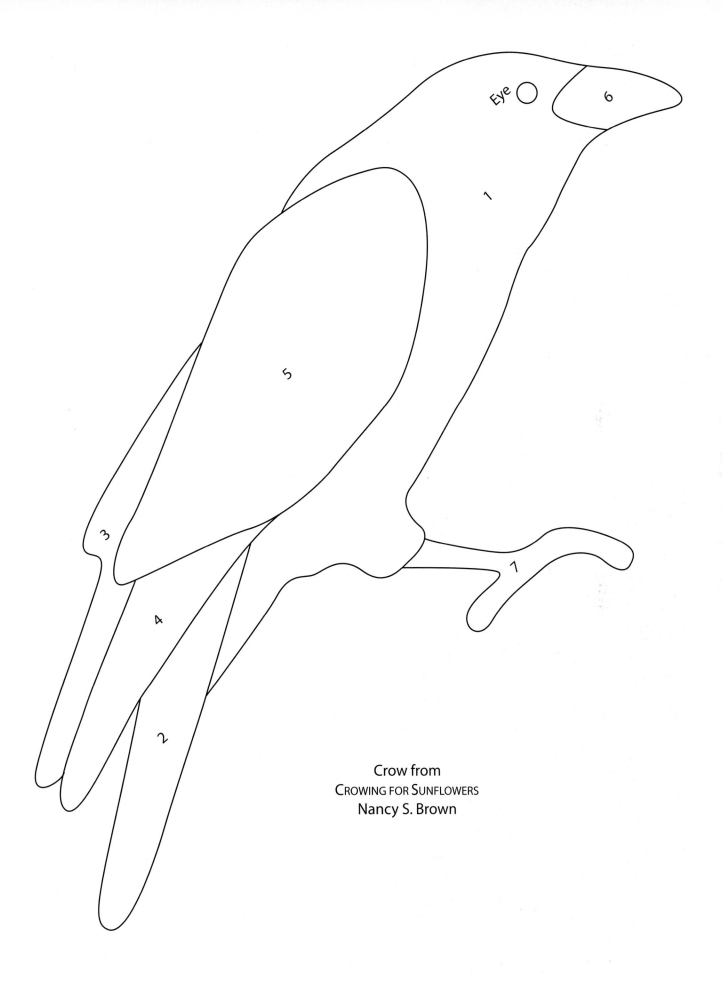

Eye

6

1

5

3

4

2

Crow from
CROWING FOR SUNFLOWERS
Nancy S. Brown

Finalist
Donnah Burke
Kirkland, Washington

Photo by Alyssa Baker

Meet Donnah

I got into quilting about eight years ago. From the start, I could not follow a simple, straightforward pattern. I always imagined it a little different. I love designing my own quilts and then trying to figure out how to "make it happen." Luckily for me, I am blessed with people around me who really love and support my work.

My three children have always made me feel that anything I did was miraculous. They, along with my two daughters-in-law and stepdaughter, are always interested in what I am working on and offer opinions that show me they take it as seriously as I do. My mother, who used to stop the car and point out a unique tree or a beautiful sunset, is generous with her praise.

Most of all, I am lucky to have a husband who provides a sounding board for new ideas, and the space and time for my projects. No problem that a full-size, unassembled quilt is lying in the middle of the living room for a week while I tweak the arrangement. Sorry that the garage is unavailable because I am dyeing cloth. I need one more yard of that fabric we bought in the quilt shop 80 miles away? Sure, we can jump in the car and get it. All these people have all allowed me to become the quilter I am.

People say, "Where do you get your ideas?" or "How did you think of that?" I could say "How could I not get ideas?" Everything inspires me—my garden, a movie, the sky, a rock, a piece of music. I have so many quilts in my head, I could live to be 140 and still not get to them all. I have always believed the ability to appreciate beauty is a great gift. It is not strictly necessary for our survival as a species but God gave us this wonderful gift of perceiving beauty. For me quilting is a way of taking in this beauty, this joy, and giving it back to others. It is a lovely series of ripples that repeats and repeats.

Inspiration and Design

When I thought about a design for a sunflower quilt, capturing several aspects of the sunflower was important to me. Foremost was portraying its impressive size. I wanted to have it appear almost too big to be contained in a quilt, the way the flower is almost too big for the garden. I wanted the flower head to be reminiscent of the sun and the overall effect to recall summer—the bright clear summer sky, the heat, the freedom one feels on such perfect summer days. Freedom! One feels unlimited and bursting with enthusiasm.

I decided to concentrate only on the actual flower. By choosing a side view, I could have it "burst" through the boundaries of the quilt. I wanted the petals to have the traditional pleating of an old-fashioned sunflower quilt, and I wanted to use that traditional design in my quilting.

The Prodigal Sunflower

Fig. 1

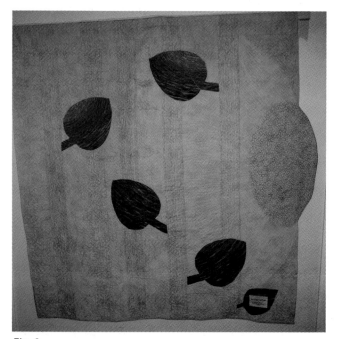

Fig. 2

I wanted the center of the flower to be intensely quilted to give the effect of seeds. The petals would be long and flowing to create a sense of movement and the color needed to shift from dark to lighter just as actual sunflower petals and flames do. To maintain the feeling of bursting free, I didn't want to have a binding on the flower, so I needed to figure out how to finish that side of the quilt while putting a traditional binding on the other three sides (fig. 1).

I wanted the quilting to have a free, natural organic look, nothing too rigid or stylized.

Since the front was all flower, I constructed the back with stems and leaves. I included the design for the sleeve so that it would blend in and I made the quilt label as a leaf (fig. 2). (Just a little quilting humor.)

Technique

Choosing fabrics is a major part of my process. I wanted a variety of fabrics in the sky blue range for the background. This is one of my favorite techniques, combining a variety of fabrics that are close in color. The different fabrics create interest, but the uniform color and value blend to give the sense of a single unit.

I decided on Ohio Star blocks interspersed with plain squares for the background. I cut squares from many different blue fabrics, spent days moving them around, standing back and gazing at the effect and then moving more squares around again. I'd leave, make a cup of coffee, come back, stare for awhile, then move some more squares. My husband would come to find me after a couple of hours and ask, "What did you do this morning?" and I'd answer, "Looked at the quilt."

To bring in the subtle shift of light in the summer sky, I chose more blues for the border. Then I added a gentle gradated blue-gray for the alternating triangles. I used the lighter gradations on the top, transitioning down the side, and used the darker ones on the bottom. I took some digital pictures of the layout and checked the camera image to see if any fabrics appeared to be disrupting a smooth transition and flow of color. I substituted strips of yellow fabric for pieces of the sky that would be covered by petals so that the blue would not shadow through and dull my flower.

For my flower, I found the perfect hand-dyed fabric for the center with blue radial lines that created a curved effect. I carefully positioned my freezer-paper template, enclosing those lines. I accentuated the lines by quilting them with shimmering blue thread (fig. 3).

For the petals, I wanted a flame-like quality. I decided I needed to dye the fabric myself. I started with white PFD (prepared for dying) cotton that I dyed a golden yellow. Then I folded the fabric shibori style, secured it with thread, and submerged the end in a bucket of beautiful reddish-brown dye. After a few minutes, I pulled it partially out of the dye and left only the very end in for a much longer time. This gave me a graduated color effect that I accentuated by quilting in several different shades of thread (figs. 4–5).

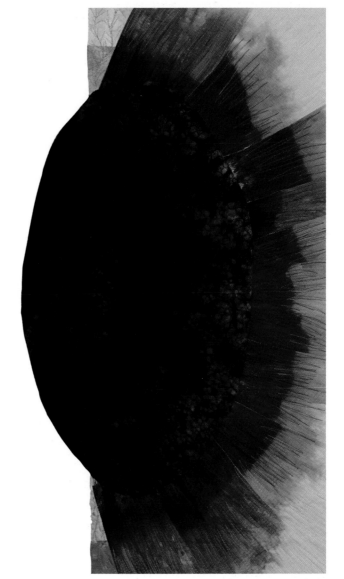

Fig. 3

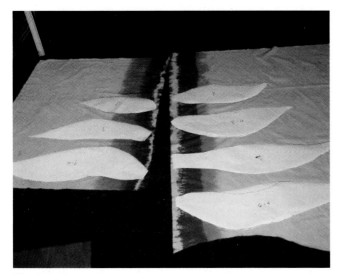

Fig. 4

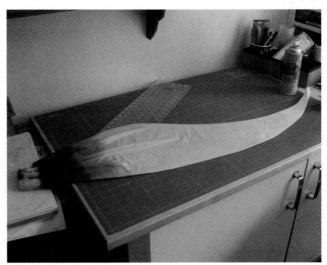

Fig. 5

Martha DeLeonardis
Katy, Texas

Photo by Angela Rodgers

Meet Martha

I cannot recall a time that I have not sewn. I always tell people that as soon as my feet could touch the floor, I was at a sewing machine. By the second grade, I was making my own clothes under my mother's tutelage, an expert seamstress herself. I started quilting around 1993 and became seriously involved in this art form after moving to Texas in 2000. I have been greatly influenced by the quilting community in the Houston area as well as by the International Quilt Festival. Had I not moved to Houston, I would probably not be creating the type of quilts I am now known for.

I started quilting because I wanted to make wallhangings for my home. Let me just say, an expert seamstress does not automatically make an expert quilter! But I quickly learned basic quilting skills and fell in love with the art form.

Initially, what I really enjoyed about quilting was that traditional quilting does not require methods such as easing and other techniques necessary for making a garment three-dimensional. It's ironic that my quilting really took off after I started to piece curves into my quilts, especially now that I am making three-dimensional quilts. I guess you can say I have conquered my aversion to dimensional techniques with a vengeance! There is one constant that hasn't changed since I started quilting: I'm still creating quilts to hang on walls.

I consider myself a "piecer" and love the idea of incorporating aspects of traditional quilt blocks into my art quilts. That is probably why I own so many books from the NQOF series. Since 2005 I have been teaching my machine-curve-piecing and other innovative piecing techniques that I translate into easy-to-understand lessons for my students.

Inspiration and Design

Last summer, I read a review of *Burgoyne Surrounded: New Quilts from an Old Favorite* that mentioned the Sunflower theme of the 2010 contest. I had been interested in this contest previously and felt I needed to revisit investigating this block. I initiated my search at The National Quilt Museum's Web site and struck gold! On the first page of the NQOF entry form was a diagram of a Sunflower block. To my pleasant surprise, the same block was used in a vintage quilt that I had recently purchased. Talk about inspiration!

The maker of the vintage quilt had pieced small petals with tucks into her flowers, one of the few methods available at that time to create a three-dimensional effect. Here was a great opportunity to turn the vintage quiltmaker's method up a notch. I wanted to utilize products available to today's quilters and bring her three-dimensional sunflower into the twenty-first century.

3-D Sunflowers 53" x 79"

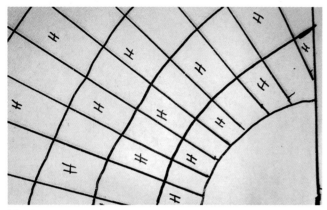

Fig. 1

Fig. 2

Fig. 3

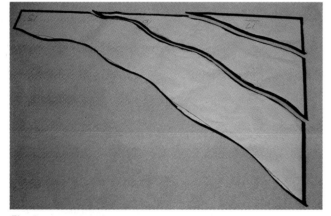

Fig. 4

I used my unique Turned Edge Fabric Weaving technique for the background. I wanted to feel as much as see light and dark value. I decided to use black-and-white fabrics exclusively in the background. I believed the lack of color would physiologically cause the viewer's "eye" to more clearly view value and bring additional emphasis to the colors used in the flowers.

I used purples for the flower centers to complement the yellows and golds of the petals. I again used my Turned Edge Fabric Weaving technique for the flower centers. It is an ideal method to incorporate curves into a "checkerboard" block set.

I considered the scale of the leaves too large to use just one fabric, and I wanted to keep the number of fabric layers to a minimum. The fused crazy-quilt technique solved the issue. I had fun experimenting with all the rarely used fancy stitches on my machine.

Technique

There are two techniques I used in this quilt that many people may not be familiar with: Turned Edge Fabric Weaving, and 3-D Construction.

I used my Turned Edge Fabric Weaving technique for the background as well as all the flower centers.

To create the full-size mirror-image pattern that is required for my weaving technique, first draw the desired image on matte acetate. A mirror image can be reproduced to the desired size by simply placing the acetate sheet upside down on the large-scale copying machine at your local commercial copier.

From the full-size mirror-image pattern (fig. 1), draw two freezer-paper patterns, one with vertical lines and the other with horizontal lines. Label one set of lines with letters, the other with numbers (figs. 2-3).

For the background, I drew straight vertical lines, and later added curves when cutting the freezer paper apart. I find I can more easily achieve gentle curves by free-form slicing the curves using an 18mm rotary cutter, rather than drawing curved lines and then cutting on the drawn line.

Iron the freezer paper sections to the wrong side of your fabric. Cut a generous ¼" seam allowance beyond the edges of the freezer paper. Snip the curved allowances, apply liquid sizing, and press the allowances back over the freezer paper (fig. 4).

To weave these sections together, lay out the vertical sections on a pressing surface and remove the freezer paper. Then, one at a time, remove the freezer paper from a horizontal section and weave it in. Apply basting glue under the overlapping weave and set with an iron. Sew the overlapping weaves now or with the quilting (fig. 5).

3-D Construction

The 3-D petals and leaves are made with two pieces of fabric layered with HeatnBond® Ultra-hold and a white-covered floral stem. Iron the layers to adhere and zigzag down the center of each shape over the floral wire. Trim the edges with a pinking rotary-cutter blade (figs. 6–8).

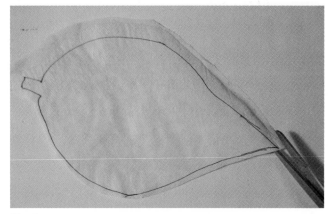

Fig. 5

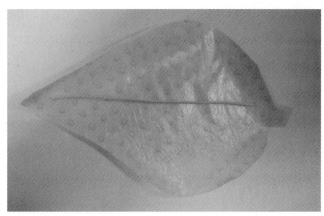

Fig. 6

Fig. 7

Fig. 8

Robin Gausebeck

Rockford, Illinois

Photo by Steven R. Gausebeck

Meet Robin

I would not be exaggerating very much to say that quilting has taken over my life! In the six years since my first quilt, made solely to fill a large blank wall space, I have

1. bought lots of gorgeous fabric that I love to look at, fold and refold, touch, and sometimes cut;
2. taken classes from wonderful quilt teachers;
3. patronized local quilt stores in every (and I mean *every*) town that I have visited on vacation;
4. gradually improved my skills by attempting new techniques in almost every quilt I design and make;
5. purchased a variety of gadgets that are so much fun to play around with;
6. become active in my quilt guild—Sinnissippi Quilters of Rockford, Illinois—where I currently serve as vice-president;
7. acquired two sewing machines that are not 35 years old and on their last legs, nor do they have plastic cams for decorative stitches;
8. managed to set up a wonderful work space where I feel challenged and inspired just by walking in the door;
9. had a quilt juried into the AQS Quilt Show & Contest in Paducah for the first time in 2009;
10. gone into withdrawal when there are days where I can't do at least 15 minutes worth of work on an in-process quilt.

I generally do not work in series—I seem to have rather eclectic tastes and so many different ideas and techniques that I want to pursue that each quilt I make turns out radically different from the ones that came before. My greatest difficulty seems to be in translating my ideas into workable and appealing designs.

I currently meet semi-regularly with a small art quilt group where I have been able to explore, on a small scale, different techniques in construction and surface design. I truly appreciate the support, advice, and honest criticism that I receive from Pam, Conny, and Karen, all of whom are wonderful quilters and great friends. I also work with some terrifically giving Unitarian Universalist quilters at my church.

My husband and I have four grown children who appreciate my quilting endeavors to varying degrees. The recent birth of our first grandchild, Charlotte Avigail, has provided an added focus for my creative energies.

Inspiration and Design

I have been fascinated by the designs of the Art Nouveau period (1890–1905) since taking an art history course in high school (and I'm not going to tell you how long ago that was!). Most of my work could be described as geometric and asymmetrical. This year's Sunflower block challenge seemed the right opportunity to work with floral motifs and a design style I admired.

Midnight in the Garden of Good and Nou'veau 56" x 56½"

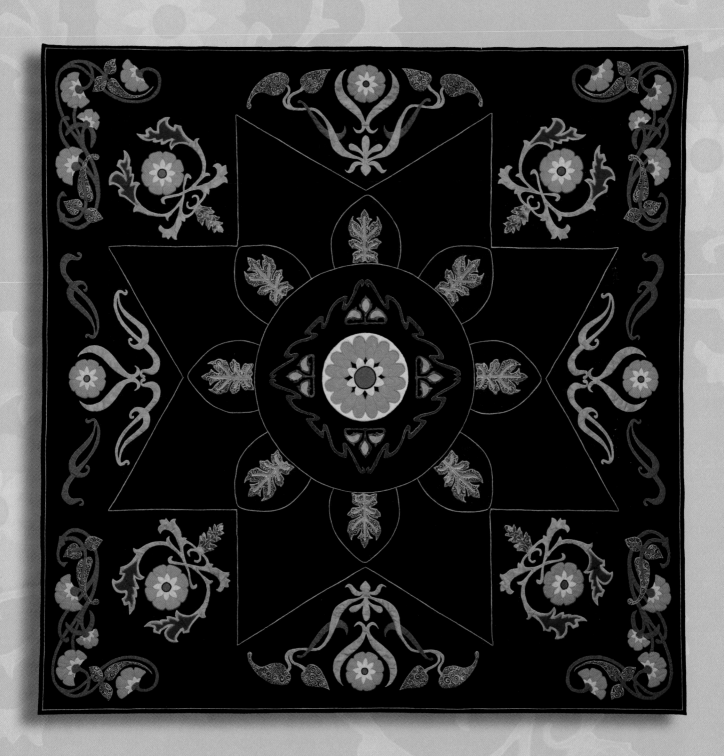

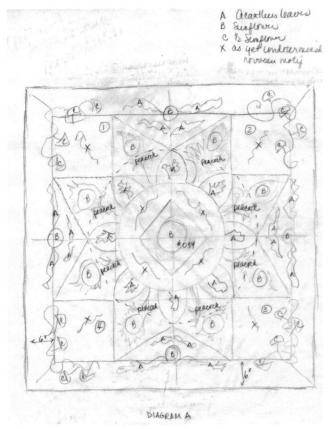

A Acanthus leaves
B Sunflower
C ½ Sunflower
X as yet undetermined nouveau motif

DIAGRAM A

Fig. 1

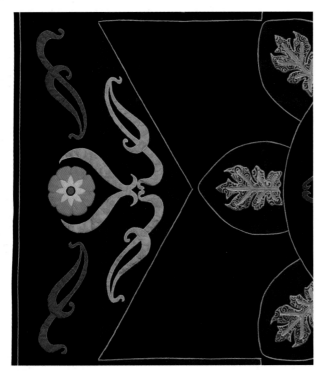

Fig. 2

The design phase of this quilt was perhaps the most fun for me. I immersed myself in my old college art and architecture history books and prowled the local libraries. I spent a lot of time experimenting with my own Art Nouveau interpretations, as well as figuring out how to modify copyright-free designs to fit my needs.

Once I decided to base the entire quilt construction on one large traditional, pieced sunflower, I needed to draft the block in a way that made for relatively easy construction. Once I had the proportions settled, I made freezer-paper templates for each shape (fig. 1).

I love the drama that incorporating black fabric in a quilt creates. It is a great canvas against which my bright fabrics really stand out and was very effective at disguising the seams in the larger pieces. Black, however, has its own limitations and drawbacks. First and foremost, it attracts every stray cat hair and piece of lint that seem to float around my studio. Second, I chose to do the majority of the machine quilting with black metallic thread—talk about tone-on-tone!

The border elements were designed to span the space where the block met border and serve as a frame to meld the two areas (fig. 2). I added piping in several of the sections to create contrast and enable the Sunflower block elements to be more readily discerned.

For the first time in this quilt, I experimented with Jane Sassaman's techniques for working with larger-scale appliqué. Rather than directly fusing all of the design elements to the base layer of the quilt, I backed entire shapes with a one-sided fusible interfacing prior to gluing, then stitched them to the quilt. This adds a slight amount of bulk to the quilt when layers are superimposed on one another, but cutting away unseen fabric from behind the designs minimizes the effect of the added layers of material. The interfacing serves to stabilize the appliqué pieces while not adding to the stiffness of the finished quilt as fusible web sometimes does.

Once my fabrics were bonded with the interfacing, I used a pair of very sharp, small scissors to cut the exact shapes. (Jane recommends using an X-Acto® knife for this process but I found that I wasn't very good at that.) Using either UHU® or Elmer's® washable glue, I adhered the shapes to the base and carefully straight-stitched around the outline of each one. This eliminated the need for cumbersome pinning. These preliminary steps were semi-permanent—it was time-consuming but possible to remove and reposition shapes that needed adjusting. The final step was satin-stitching around the edges, using a variety of decorative threads (fig. 3).

This is a technique that I would choose to use again, particularly if, like Jane Sassaman, I wanted to work with larger appliqué pieces that constituted a great portion of the quilt. I think this would lend itself well to a more improvisational style of designing, where I might create the individual elements before deciding on a final layout.

Each time my husband or I looked at the quilt, the center seemed to glow with an inner light that we just loved. We will miss having it on the wall during the time it is traveling with the NQOF exhibit.

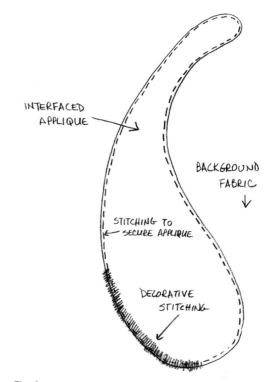

Fig. 3

Finalist
Julia Graber
Brooksville, Mississippi

Photo by Amy Graber

Meet Julia

My interest in quiltmaking was sparked in my early twenties while working as a clerk at The Clothes Line, my parents' fabric store in Dayton, Virginia. I made two very heavy woolen comforters that were pieced and tied.

I come from a large family and in recent years, four generations of the women get together for a week to 10 days to sew, quilt, and weave baskets, talk, and laugh. We take turns preparing two meals a day—a brunch and supper.

Mother (center) and her girls

Grandmother Vera Heatwole has had a lot of influence on me and our family. She pieced a "Velvet" comforter in the four-patch style with black sashing and red cornerstones. This inspired my mother, Margaret Heatwole, to make one just like it, which in turn inspired me, a lot of my sisters, and a niece to each make one of our own.

"Velvet" comforter

I came to Mississippi from the beautiful Shenandoah Valley of Virginia in my early 20s to teach at the Magnolia Mennonite Christian Day School for our church. It was here that I met and married Paul Graber.

After I was married, I made my UGLIEST quilt. What was I thinking? I guess I wanted to use up scraps. Since I had a lot of the flannel back, why not just fold it around to the front to make the top bigger?

UGLIEST

We live on a farm raising hogs and grain and have a small trucking company hauling locally. We are also involved in church activities and mission work in Romania.

We have five sons and one daughter. Although Joel's wife, Sheila, is blind, she and I made a Bow Tie quilt together. I cut out the blocks and she sewed them together by feel, using a couple of layers of masking tape taped to the right side of the presser foot and taking ½" seams.

Bow Tie

Our daughter Amy helps in the office of our trucking business. She made a sampler quilt when she was 16. I made RAGAMUFFIN II for her son, Ashton.

RAGAMUFFIN II

Next is Quinten, married to Evie. FEATHERED STARS IN BLUES was made for their wedding. They have given us two grandchildren, Kirby and Stacy, and of course I made quilts for them, too.

FEATHERED STARS IN BLUE

Our next son, Brian, was killed in October 2004 in a motorcycle accident when he was 20.

Dustin is in college but still helps on the farm. \Craig, our youngest, drives a truck for us. I made CHRISTMAS SPLENDOR as a wedding gift when he married Angie.

CHRISTMAS SPLENDOR

The Contest

This year is not my first time entering the New Quilts from an Old Favorite contest. The first time was the year the block was Monkey Wrench. No Shadow of Turning got a rejection letter. But that didn't stop me from entering the next year using the Seven Sisters block.

Because I am number three of seven sisters, it seemed right for me to enter that one. Our Heatwole family is a strong family unit (represented by the bright block of stars near the center of the quilt). One by one we got married and left the family nest, going in different directions (the bright stars flinging out from the center), and settled in different places around the country; hence the name, Seven Sisters—Leaving Home.

In 2004 A Plate of Pineapples won 4th place. The next two years, my quilts were finalists, and last year my Bubbled Burgoyne placed 5th.

A Plate of Pineapples

Seven Sisters—Leaving Home

Bubbled Burgoyne

Design

I used Electric Quilt® 6 software to design the Sunburst Beauty block with a Carpenter's Wheel setting. The same design appears in the square and diamond blocks, with a different orientation in the diamonds. I used single-fabric spikes instead of piecing them.

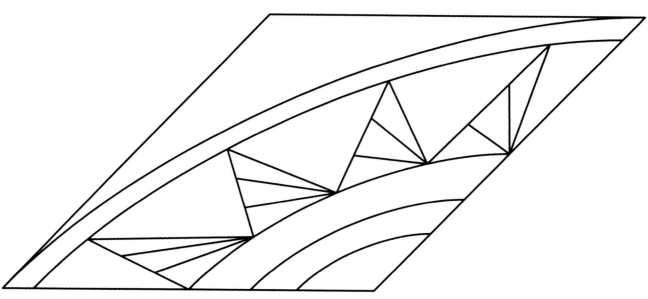

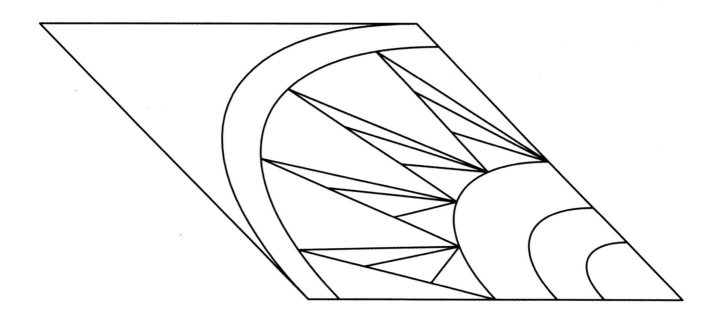

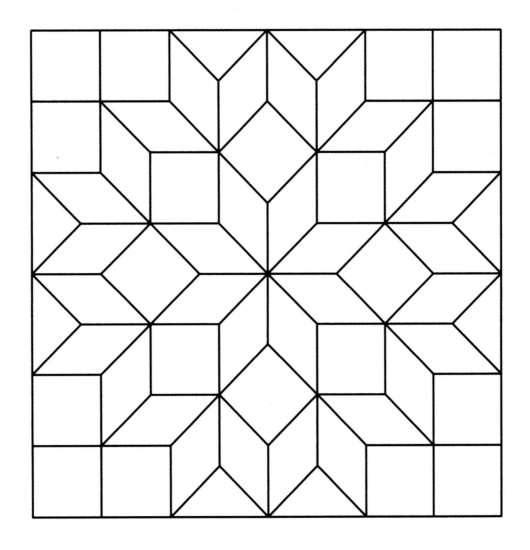

Finalist

Mary Ann Herndon

The Woodlands, Texas

Photo by John C. Herndon, Jr.

Meet Mary Ann

Like most quilters, I have explored many art forms, but it is quilting that has allowed me to grow and stay motivated to continue learning new techniques and create new projects. From my first quilting class with Karey Bresenhan's mother at Great Expectations to the present time, quilting has been an endeavor that, fortunately now, I can choose to do without any guilt. I have retired from a full-time job as director of libraries for a local school district, my three children all have their own lives and children of their own, and my husband of 54 years is semi-retired and content with his own interests and non-elaborate meals.

Color, design, and texture are the three elements in quilting that continue to inspire me to plan more pieces than I will ever have time to complete. The combination of other art mediums and the wealth of so many talented quilt artists greatly influence my work. Color in any bright shade fills my studio shelves, as well as gradated and hand-dyed fabrics. Design in most pieces incorporates both some traditional and some contemporary aspects. This is the area in which I need the most help. I now understand how important math should have been to me in my college classes.

Judged shows continue to motivate me to create work that the viewer will be compelled to look at and then turn around and take a deeper look. I have been fortunate to place in several contests and have had quilts featured on magazine covers and in books. My biggest problem in entering quilts is procrastinating to the last moment, resulting in late nights and large postage fees.

Inspiration and Design

The New Quilts from an Old Favorite contest is one that I particularly look forward to entering because it requires the quilter to delve into the past while reaching for the contemporary. I welcome this challenge since my appreciation for quilting, although rooted in the traditional designs, has evolved into a preference for quilts that contain some of both worlds.

As I approached the sunflower planning, I realized that choosing just one version of the Sunflower pattern would be problematic since there were many similar blocks, as noted in compilations by Jinny Beyer and Barbara Brackman. So, I decided I needed to find a showcase for several of my favorites. After sifting through folders of "ideas to use one day," I found two that led to FLORA. The first was in a book by Anita Lobel in which all the people depicted are made of food or objects. The second was an advertisement from a Las Vegas casino that included a girl clothed in flowers. From that point, it was a matter of choosing the specific blocks, the background, and the fabric.

Flora 72½" x 71"

The biggest challenge was the background. I planned for a yellow to radiate out from the center to the edges. In trying to achieve this shading, there were all sorts of problems with shape, etc., which I finally managed to massage with some seaming and steaming. The final result was worth all the manipulations because when I hung it up, the block silhouette and the vibrant flowers really made an impact against the background that I had worried with so much.

Technique

Flora has two main parts: (1) the background and (2) the flower-filled silhouette. The background was pieced as a Log Cabin block although there are easier ways to achieve a background that radiates from light to dark. Choosing fabrics that would contrast with the dark silhouette and the flowers as well as ones that had highlights rather than just being solid was key to making a more vibrant piece. I drew a silhouette shape, enlarged it, cut it out of paper, and transferred it to fabric.

I researched Sunflower patterns, chose several, and enlarged them to different sizes, adding some detail shapes to fill some spaces (fig. 1). The Nadelstern stripe I used for the binding led to the colors I chose for the flowers. Paula's symmetrical designs were perfect choices for most of the flowers since many Sunflower patterns lend themselves to the kaleidoscopic technique where each petal is cut from the matching pattern in the fabric. This is where a repeat pattern fabric is helpful.

For the other flowers, I enlarged the pattern, made my own templates, and did some paper piecing where possible. In all cases, I eliminated the block's square border. Jenny Beyer's book *Patchwork Patterns*, especially the pages on drawing the Mariner's Compass and Sunflower designs, was an invaluable aid in drafting some of the sunflowers.

FIG. 1

Basically, you draw a circle the size you want it to be, draw a fat center circle, draw a second circle midway between the middle and outer circles, and divide the circle into 16 or 32 divisions. Then draw diamond shapes in the outer two circles using the division fold lines as guides (figs. 2–4).

Appliqué techniques included needle-turn and some facing and turning of smaller appliqué shapes. Cutting out the layers beneath all the appliqués made the quilting much easier. To enhance the flower girl, I quilted the background in a diagonal grid and outlined all the large pieces and quilted around and inside all the flower parts. Blank background spaces were filled with random quilting shapes.

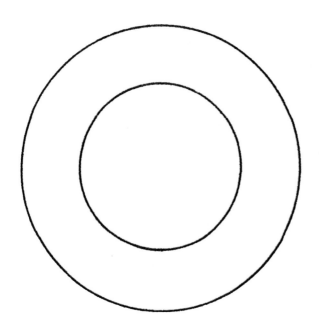

FIG. 2

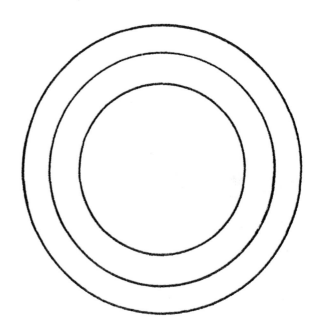

FIG. 3

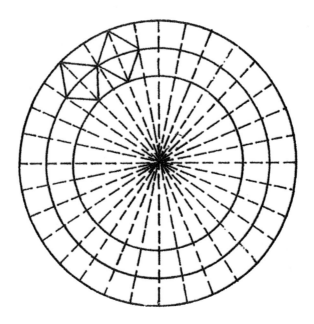

FIG. 4

Finalist
Patricia Hobbs
Macomb, Illinois

Photo by John K. Hobbs

Meet Patricia

I began sewing my own clothes at age ten. The neighborhood girls were dying fabric with watercolors in my garage at about the same time. We made doll clothes and blankets to trade within our group. By about age fourteen, I had read quilting books and began experimenting with historic quilting techniques like English paper piecing. It was easy to move into making baby quilts for gifts.

My background is in art education. I taught art in the public school system for 34 years. After I retired five years ago, I joined the Prairie Quilters' Guild. This was the turning point where quilting became "fiber art" and I began making art quilts of my own design. My attendance at the American Quilter's Society quilt shows, attending workshops, and entering quilt contests and guild challenges helped to make my quilts more professional in quality.

My mother gave me an unevenly pieced wool "hap" top (a utility quilt for warmth, not beauty). When I finally began to work on this quilt, it had moth holes. I appliquéd a wool scene over the top and used needle felting to add shading. Even though my mother had passed away, I felt like we had worked together on this quilt. I know that she would have been pleased with our finished project.

Quilts are my venue for communication and expressing ideas. I work on more than one proj-ect at a time; I have three or four new designs in my head, and a log book of future quilts. My method of working takes me into the late hours of the night when phones no longer ring and there is peace and quiet needed to think.

Inspirations and Design

I printed off the contest rules right after the AQS quilt show in April. I had thoughts of revisiting my PRAIRIE SONG quilt, made for my guild's "Little Quilt on the Prairie" challenge. It featured paper-pieced sunflowers and a large pieced sunflower, but I dislike doing anything twice and piecing the sunflower center had been painful.

PRAIRIE SONG

I decided to distort the original sunflower pattern as it wasn't *my* "old favorite." The real inspiration for my quilt came from my own garden lily pond (fig. 1, page 66). Sunflowers grow all around the pond wherever they choose to pop up, providing late-summer color.

FIG. 1

FIG. 2

I was visiting my friend Judy Witten, and she showed me a queen-size quilt that her mother, Sara Carlberg, had made in 1999 (fig. 2). Judy and her grandmother, Edna Lantz, hand quilted it. I realized it was the traditionally pieced Sunflower pattern. It was the first time I had seen the pattern made into a quilt and it made the pattern seem very real to me.

After looking at a photograph of my garden full of sunflowers, I did a sketch that I thought might be fun to make. I hand-colored the sketch with colored pencils to make it bright, playful, and cheerful (fig. 3).

Technique

My very first quilt (not yet finished) was a Grandmother's Flower Garden with English paper-pieced hexagons. Now, fifty years later, I was making the same hexagons for the background of my sunflower quilt. This time, I printed hexagons onto manila folders and cardstock.

The quilt was done in three horizontal bands: the dirt, the sunflowers, and the sky. The dirt or ground was hexagons with additional hills pieced in above them (fig. 4).

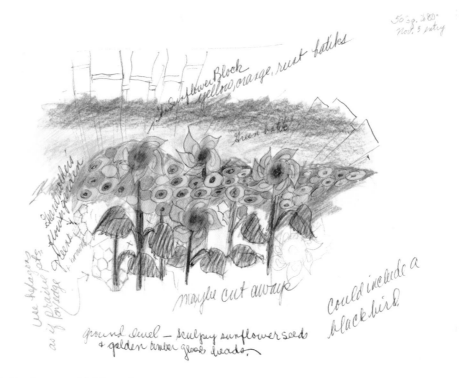

FIG. 3

The next band contains the machine appliquéd sunflowers, leaves, and stems and links this quilt to the traditional Sunflower pattern (fig. 5). The stems extend down over the ground band off the bottom edge of the quilt, joining the two sections. The third band is the sky. Each section was labeled with a sequential number and color notation. Some of the sunflower petals overlap the sky band linking these two sections together.

The machine quilting was completed on the bottom section first. All cardstock pieces, except those in the outside edge border of the hexagons, had been removed. The random quilting pattern represents a rooting seedling. It was done with brown thread and stitched up to the last row of hexagons around the edge of the quilt. The backing of the quilt was trimmed ¼" from the edge of the outside border hexagons.

The batting was trimmed evenly with the border hexagons. The edges of the hexagons were hand sewn to the backing, turning the backing raw edges in ¼". As each piece was sewn, the basting thread was pulled, and the cardstock hexagon was slipped out. The green band was quilted in a matching green thread with a meandering pattern. The sunflowers were quilted in concentric lines with matching thread. The sky band was quilted with a neutral blue thread in lines radiating out from the central vanishing point.

The binding was sewn on in sections to match the sky, green growing area, and brown ground. The final sunflower was made separately from the rest of the quilt and then tacked onto the edge of the quilt (fig. 6).

No garden is complete without crows. They eat the seeds from flowers and scatter them in places where the gardener did not plant them nor intend for them to grow. Crows are known as tricksters in Native American culture, often teaching humans how to fit in with the natural world.

FIG. 4

FIG. 5

FIG. 6

Finalist

Ann Horton

Redwood Valley, California

Photo by Jessica Horton

Meet Ann

I believe our environment—both external and the inner emotional life—affects our creative endeavors in all ways. Living in the northern California coastal mountains, I am influenced by the natural beauty of vast horizons of misty mountains, meadows of wildflowers, and wildlife on all sides. Our Mendocino County has a rich heritage of native Pomo basket making, Wild West stories, coastal beauty, and people who seek refuge and renewal in our peaceful valleys. Soaring redwood trees, rugged coastal vistas, oak-studded valleys, and small rural communities all add to the abundance that is reflected in my art. My inner geography includes my love of music, art, faith, friendship, family, and my work as a psychotherapist.

My quilting life embraces this life with zest, and I have a jolly good time exploring each new work with a sense of wonder for the blessings of a life deeply experienced. While my immediate environs influence me, I am also fascinated with other cultures and the textile history of their people. Every quilt is another opportunity to explore and evolve.

Inspiration and Design

In the summer of 2008, my daughter, Jessica, spent a good deal of time in Guatemala and Mexico, researching visual arts and culture for her graduate work. She came home for a visit, bringing a beautiful stack of Guatemalan fabrics for her fabric-hungry mother. While I was smitten with the beauty and explosion of colors represented by these incredible hand-loomed textiles, I was aware that an even greater gift was given me through the stories and descriptions my daughter shared of her visits with the women weaving in remote rural areas who worked to make these beautiful pieces of art.

Weaving hands. Photo by Jessica Horton.

Poverty, challenges to meet basic living needs, education, health care for their families—so much to think about as I touched the work of their hands. These Guatemalan fabrics have crossed borders to be celebrated throughout the world, yet the weavers themselves are so often locked into a cycle of poverty and poor compensation for their art. As a textile lover and artist myself, I feel a huge sense of compassion

Southern Borders

70" x 70"

and concern, yet I am frustrated by my limited ability to help bring about change. I believe all of us who love textiles need to be aware of the challenges these ethnic fabrics represent.

While working with the fabrics and adding the beautiful embroideries to represent the tile work (fig. 1), crafted figurines, and embroidery of the Latino culture, I thought long and hard about the borders we all erect to contain and protect our own lives.

These same borders can confine and trap others in more helpless positions. I decided that my quilt would reflect all of these thoughts. A tall order! In the end, the quilt is a happy, sunny statement. Celebrate Love! Celebrate Friendship! Celebrate Families! And please, remember the challenges the weaving women of Guatemala face.

FIG. 1. Mexican tiled doorway. Photo by Jessica Horton.

FIG. 2

The decision to make the quilt in a medallion format seemed natural. An expanded, glorious Sunflower block suggested the circle of life and set the stage for borders to come. I almost always utilize digitized embroidery in my work and worked with my software to fussy-shape a huge variety of motifs into the softly flowing corner embroideries surrounding the sunflower medallion.

The next border was great fun to create. I shaped designs to form the "tiles" that started to convey a message of friendship. I used a wonderful appliqué design of a large sunflower, eliminating some of the original design, adding more bits of Guatemalan fabric to the quilt. Variegated threads added colorful zing to the designs.

To pull it all together, I cut multiple small squares of the fabrics and pieced it to surround the tiles with color and warmth. The final red Guatemalan border provides one more venue for the border embroidery and beading. These little highlights add interest, more color and movement, as well as that all-important texture I love about this quilt.

The quilting was a challenge. I used very fine machine quilting in the center background (fig. 2) and on the tiles and hand quilted the Guatemalan textiles with heavy perle cotton. The contrast complemented the hand-woven fabrics while helping the embroideries to "pop." A bit of red cotton cording around the tiles and center also gave additional zing factor. The final binding was carefully cut from a woven fabric to provide a beautiful line of design for the very last border.

Technique—The Challenge of Using Unusual Fabrics

Much of my quilting work utilizes textured, thick, irregular fabrics not often seen in quilts (fig. 3). I take every opportunity to search for these wonderful fabrics when I am out in the world. While some of these textiles are soft and drape well, others are rather stiff and thick with tightly woven threads—a challenge to mix! In SOUTHERN BORDERS, it is definitely the richness of these fabrics that makes the quilt work. So how did I do it?

The biggest challenge was the center medallion. All those diamonds cut on the bias were going to be a headache. The best words here were *slow* and *gentle*.

I handled the fabrics very carefully, set my machine to piece with a light pressure foot to minimize stretch, and used 60-weight thread to reduce bulk (fig. 4). After the sunflower medallion was pieced I laid it on my background fabric and hand sewed it into place, shaping as I went. I faced the inner turquoise circle I had fussy cut from striped fabric (fig. 5).

The very center of the medallion was placed under the turquoise ring and hand quilted in place with French knots. They, along with the beads, added texture.

Hand quilting the medallion gave me another opportunity to work gently with the fabric so as not to stretch the textiles. All the Guatemalan fabrics were hand quilted with the perle cotton. I wanted the hand quilting to show and I used a lovely variegated cotton perle thread to highlight the array of colors in the pieced border. When I hand-sewed the ceramic beads in place, I also used the colored threads. The simple design rule of repetition with variation came into play here with the quilting and beading.

The lure of ethnic textiles and the people and cultural heritage they represent will continue to entice me. Collecting the fabrics and envisioning their use in quilts is a worthy endeavor. Rising to the challenge they present is rewarding when the end result pays tribute to the origins of the fabrics as well as the artistry of the quilter. And so the journey continues.

Fig. 3. Woven Guatemalan textiles. Photo by Jessica Horton.

FIG. 4

FIG. 5

Learn more about Ann on her Web site:
www.annhortonquilts.com

Finalists

Wendy Rieves
Brookfield, Wisconsin

Chris Lynn Kirsch
Watertown, Wisconsin

Photo by Sears Portrait Studio

Meet the Quilters

Chris

My mom taught me to sew as a child. Thirty years later my sister-in-law talked me into taking a quilting class. In between I married my high school sweetheart (who is still my best friend), had two children, and worked as a dental hygienist. Since then my passions are my family and this wonderful addiction called quilting.

I began as a very traditional quilter, with no background in art. Within a few years I discovered I love teaching quiltmaking and I've had the delightful opportunity to author two books. The next part of the adventure was realizing I could actually design and create fiber art. It is still difficult for me to believe that my quilts are award-winning.

I've come to understand that quilting is a gift the Lord has given me and each step in my journey is planned by Him for a reason. My quilting has been the anchor in my life during difficult times. It has also taken me many places and allowed me to form meaningful friendships. In recent times I've sensed the Lord asking me what I'm doing for Him and I find that the quilts I make with faith as inspiration turn out to be my best work.

Wendy

I have loved crafts and sewing all my life. I started quilting in 1989 when I was laid off from a job as an occupational therapist. I thought I would save some money by making my own king-size quilt and have something to do with my time (as if taking care of two small boys was not enough!). I certainly didn't save any money but I sure did find something to do with my time!

I have a very understanding husband, four children, and a dog. I live in the same city I grew up in so I am near my family, longtime friends, and church. I love quilting because of what a varied art it is. There is room for the exacting personality as well as the free spirit.

I have a passion for teaching. I get to see my original patterns made up in various colorways. I try to encourage my students to make each quilt their own by varying the design, adding to the design, or just using it as a jumping off point. It is exciting to see a student who has taken the information presented and made it their own.

The Collaboration

In the mid 1990s we met at a quilt guild meeting. Shortly after we met we attended quilt week in Paducah and discovered we travel very well together. When we had the opportunity to lead a quilting cruise on the Mississippi River, we jumped at it. We have been fortunate enough to take groups of quilters on other cruises. We tell our students, "Nurture your creativity—you never know where it is going to take you!"

To learn more about our quilting adventures, please visit www.chrisquilts.net.

Welcoming the Son Into Our Garden 50" x 59"

We have such fun together, it's surprising to us that we haven't done a quilt collaboration until now. But, the Lord's timing is perfect and WELCOMING THE SON INTO OUR GARDEN was the right first quilt for us.

Quilts are such blessed evidence of time well spent. It is satisfying to know that quilts will live into the future and be seen, used, and appreciated by others. We hope that people who look at our quilt will be inspired and appreciate all that God's creative spirit has to offer.

Inspiration and Design

Wendy

Sunflowers hold a special place in my heart. At kindergarten registration over the years, each of my kids received sunflower seeds. The teacher would tell the excited children to plant the seeds and when the flowers bloomed it would be time for school. We loved watching them grow. They have come to symbolize new beginnings and how much of what we do in life is planting seeds and then watching and waiting for the mature plant to show its pretty face.

I love the Fibonacci design in the seed head of the sunflower. To create that in fabric, I realized that photo transfer would be appropriate for a contest whose theme was new from old. What would our foremothers think about photo transfer in quilts!

I put the fairies in the quilt to add a beating heart. They are shaded with crayon, as are the sunflower petals. They are there to show that the seeds and plants need a little nourishment and help from outside themselves. In going through life, we cannot do it all on our own. We need God, family, and friends.

Chris

After Wendy raw-edge appliquéd her sunflowers to a batik background, she gave them to me. I looked through my encyclopedia of quilt blocks and discovered there were many Sunflower blocks, so I made a bunch.

I drafted and paper pieced the sun using my own Mariner's Compass folded-paper technique. The sky seemed to need more interest, so that's where I added the Sunflower blocks. I returned the top to Wendy and she added her delightful fairies and did some thread painting and quilting on the flowers. When it was once again my turn I used a type of trapunto to add dimension to the quilted rays of the sun and filled in everything else with fun, free-motion quilting.

There are many things I like about this quilt. It is such a joyful scene. I love Wendy's fairies and the combination of blue and yellow has always been a favorite of mine, but I think what I really like best about this quilt is how it is a symbol of our friendship, our passion for quilting, and our mutual faith.

Technique: Wendy's Fairies

I drew the fairy in reverse onto Wonder-Under® web and fused it to a very light colored batik. I colored the details on the fabric with regular Crayola® crayons. The paper-backed fusible stabilizes the fabric for coloring. The batik fabric automatically helps me with the shading because of the light and dark areas within the batik. I once learned in a painting class how important purple is for shading, so I always use purple in my fairies. The fairy came alive as her dress, hair, and wings were colored in. I added a little more detail with a Pigma® pen.

When choosing fabric for the bubble or aura behind the fairy, I looked at my messy cutting area, and there was a piece of fusible interfacing on the top of the heap! I cut out a 4" circle and fused the bubble and the fairy onto the background fabric. I did some thread painting on her and added some glitter glue. The fairy was ready to take flight and get to work!

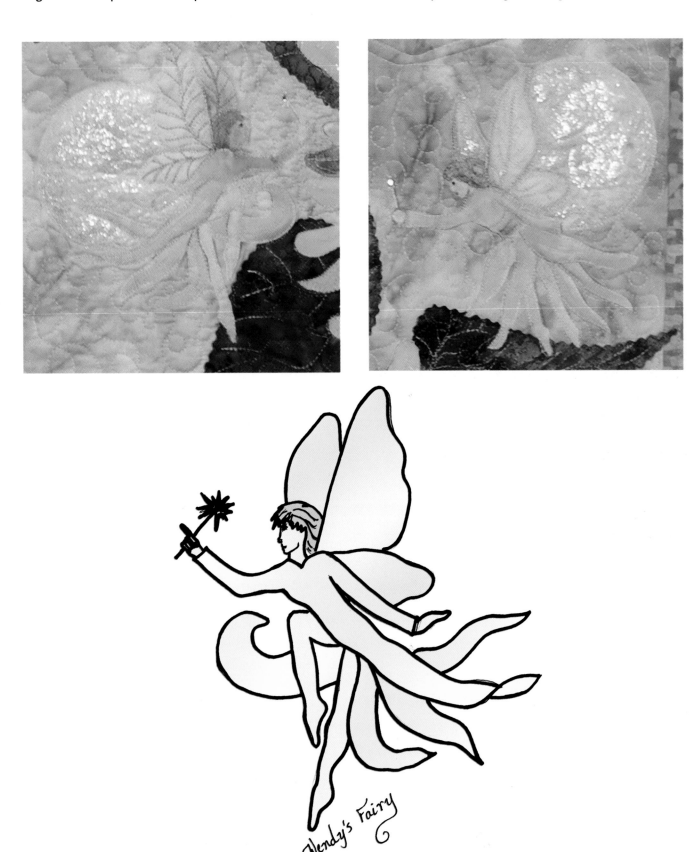

Wendy's Fairy

Finalist
Theresea Reeves
Oberlin, Kansas

Photo by James L. Reeves

Meet Theresea

I was raised and continue to live in Northwest Kansas. As a small child I remember watching my mother make clothes for my sisters and me. I was fascinated at the process of cutting the pieces of cloth and then sewing them back together in a pattern to make a beautiful garment. Along with Mom's help I completed two years of garment construction in high school home economics classes. The skills I learned helped me later in life with my own family, making baby clothes for my sons. I will never forget the little white shirt I made them with an embroidered red rocking horse on the back yoke. It wasn't until 1993 that I found quilting. I totally enjoy every aspect of quiltmaking and I especially love the challenge of accuracy.

I have operated a longarm quilting business for the last six years. Owning my own machine lets me experiment with new quilting designs and helps me be creative in many different ways. It has also let me work on quilts made by everyone from rank amateurs to truly gifted and dedicated quilters. By seeing what others do right and wrong I have been able to build on that and improve my own skills. I am a member of a quilt guild in McCook, Nebraska, whose members keep me inspired and challenged.

In 1997 I placed 2nd in a Keepsake Quilting contest. The quilt I entered was based on a Christmas theme and was also an original design. I have entered my quilts in many local and regional quilt shows in my area. I also enjoy oil painting and knitting in my spare time. I took art classes at McCook Junior College for two years and the skills I learned there were put to use in the fabric painting I did on No Forwarding Address. By managing my time quite well I will continue to operate my longarm quilting business and also design additional original quilts.

Inspiration and Design

My study of art has opened a new outlook on quilting. My goal in making this quilt was not only to put a new twist on an old favorite, but to also apply basic art principles to create a quilt with a three-dimensional appearance. I wanted my quilt to look realistic. Since the sunflower is the Kansas state flower, it seemed only natural to put in a landscape. They appear everywhere in the fields, pastures, and ditches of my native area of Kansas. As the elderly farmers pass away and their land is consolidated into bigger and bigger farms, more and more of the farmsteads are abandoned and their mailboxes are a testimony to their demise.

I was inspired to do this quilt as a tribute to the changing times when I saw a row of neglected mailboxes surrounded by weeds, grass, and sunflowers. I dedicate this to the farmers who came before us, the farmers who carry on, and the Kansas State Sunflower that tells us some things will never change.

No Forwarding Address 64½" x 65"

Techniques

I used needle-turn hand appliqué on the sky, ground, mailboxes, and sunflowers in the center square, which is set on point. I determined how large I wanted the center square before deciding on the borders. I used graph paper to draw a 33" x 33" grid and freehand sketched in the three mailboxes, set at different angles to give them an abandoned look (fig. 1).

I freehand sketched in the sunflowers and stems, drawing on my experience doing oil painting (fig. 2). All of the flowers are slightly different and the petals are placed at different angles to give the effect of wind as it moves them. No two sunflowers will look alike, so if you trace over a picture or use a projector to trace you will not get the natural appearance of the wild sunflowers.

Here is where knowing a few basic art principles came in handy. The sky is lighter at the horizon and gradually gets darker as you move away from the horizon. I chose eight different sky fabrics ranging from light to dark in value. The light fabrics at the horizon are also narrower and become wider as you work to the darker values overhead. I used freezer-paper templates pressed to the right side of the fabric for all the needle-turn hand appliqué.

The ground was worked the same as the sky, using eight fabrics ranging from light to dark, with the lightest fabric starting at the horizon and working down the quilt to the darkest value at the bottom. This gives the quilt depth and realism.

Establishing a light source is very important as it determines where you put your shadows, which gives your quilt a three-dimensional appearance. My light is coming from the top right. I chose medium-value fabrics for both the mailboxes and sunflowers. This allowed me to add both light and dark shading, mixing different values of fabric ink. When inking fabric, iron

FIG. 1

FIG. 2

freezer paper to the wrong side of the fabric to stabilize it. After the inking is completed remove the freezer paper and set the ink with an iron.

I chose medium-value fabrics for the leaves, stems, and petals. The center and petals of each sunflower are individually inked according to the light source and hand appliquéd to the quilt. I also cut a duplicate of each petal for a lining and layered it underneath the inked petal to prevent seams from showing through. This greatly enhanced the appearance of the sunflowers. You will notice some of the flowers and leaves go beyond the muslin background. They were finished after the 5" black border was added. This brings the flowers and leaves out of the box and imparts life and dimension to an otherwise flat surface.

I embellished the design by adding bees, lady-bugs, and a spider and web using silk ribbon and embroidery floss. I also added colonial knots to the sunflower heads to give the texture of seeds. The black border was mitered, the corners were filled in with 2" squares, and a final 4" border was added.

Developing a light source was the most important step in the construction of this quilt. The machine quilting was done freehand and the quilted grasses and weeds among the sunflowers in the foreground, I feel, add to the abandoned look. The yellow quilting thread in the 2" squares and border extends the yellow from the sunflowers in the center of the quilt. This helps pull the quilt together and lets the color flow throughout.

Finalist

Karen R. Watts

Houston, Texas

Photo by Mark J. Ferring

Meet Karen

Over the past 18 years, quilting has been a huge part of my life. Like many quilters, I had always dabbled with other crafts. I always felt better about spending my days as an accountant if I could also spend some time, no matter how little, creating. When I discovered quilting in 1991, I gave up the other hobbies, as quilting immediately became a passion. The following year, after my daughter was born, I stopped working outside the home.

Quilting gave balance to the sometimes intense job of raising an autistic son and gifted daughter. Having the ability to disappear into the sewing room and become immersed in designing, playing with beautiful fabric, or simply mindless strip piecing was essential to my sanity. Of course, both kids spent much time in there with me, as playing with scraps was a favorite pastime.

This has been a year of transition, and next year will be even more so. After being a mom first and a quilter second, the roles are shifting. My son, who is 22, has had his own apartment for six months. My daughter is a senior in high school at the top of her class. They are completely different, and I am so proud of both of them in so many ways. We spent the summer getting Brian settled in his apartment and visiting colleges with Gina. She has her own car now, so I'm not a chauffeur any longer.

In between all this, I managed to spend some time at our place in the mountains of southern New Mexico. My husband and I plan to move there permanently in 2010 after Gina goes off to college. Of course, this means retirement for him and a new quilt studio for me! It will be a separate building, so I can design it to meet my needs.

If someone asks what my favorite part of quilting is, I have to answer, "I love it all!" I have many, many designs and variations that will never be made, simply because it was fun to draw them. I love all kinds of piecing, and then there is quilting. I enjoy developing a quilting plan for a quilt and then getting it done. I especially like when it turns out how I wanted it to (which isn't always the case, needless to say).

Lately I've been trying to finish several quilts for my guild's community service project. For several years we've been donating lap quilts to The Rose, a breast cancer diagnostic and treatment center where all women are served, regardless of their ability to pay. Each woman who is diagnosed with breast cancer receives a quilt from us.

Inspiration and Design

I have always loved the Southwest—the culture, the art, the beautiful scenery, and especially the Navajo world view. This view sees the universe as an all-inclusive whole in which everything has its place with a unique and

Navajo Sunflower 58" x 71"

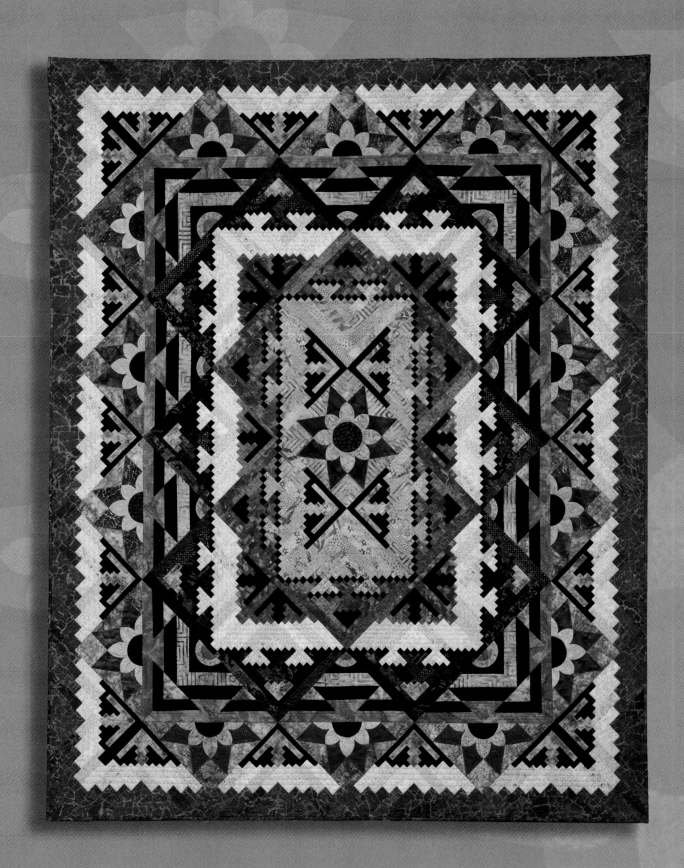

beneficial relationship to all other living things. The Navajos' spiritual beliefs are based on *Hózhó*, which means existing in a state of balance, harmony, wellness, peace, and completeness. Simply being at our place gives me that feeling of balance and harmony. It was there that it came to me that I should make my sunflower quilt in the style of a Navajo rug or weaving.

I had my laptop, with EQ6 ready and waiting! I started drawing blocks that had a Navajo "flavor," using some pictures in my *New Mexico Magazine* for inspiration. The coloring I chose is certainly not traditional, but then I am not Navajo. By far the most difficult block in this quilt is this one, which I refer to as the Navajo block. In fact, when I tried to make one it was not even close to square! It's based on a half-inch grid, and has approximately 118 pieces.

I decided to fuse some of the elements in order to simplify them and stitch the fused pieces with a blanket stitch, in keeping with my rug look.

I liked the look of the blanket stitch so well that I also fused my Sunflower blocks. The other side of the half-sunflower was paper pieced.

The design was not finalized until just a few months before the deadline. I was working on the blocks, but kept changing the center of the quilt. I also wasn't sure how the edge of the outer blocks would be finished. Then I found the perfect piece of fabric and redesigned the blocks to incorporate the new fabric. Sometimes it's just serendipity!

Technique

I'm not a huge fan of fusing, but sometimes it's necessary to get the effect you want. Here are some of my tips for successful fusing.

I use a very lightweight fusible web to minimize stiffness, but it must be stitched down. I cut away the inside of the shape, leaving a ¼" of fusible inside my drawn line. If the piece is very small, or has many skinny parts, I leave the whole piece of web intact. Choosing a contrasting thread or a decorative stitch can add visual interest. I chose to use the blanket stitch and Sulky® threads that matched the fabric.

I drew my Sunflower block in EQ6, slightly modifying the old design shown on the New

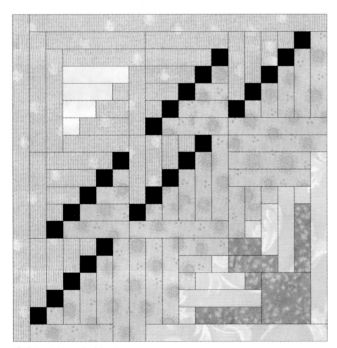

Original Navajo block

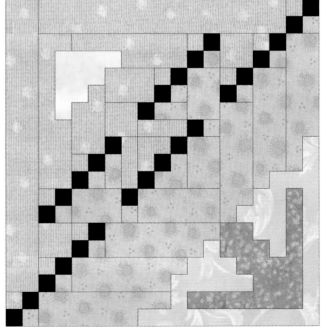

Simplified Navajo block

Quilts from an Old Favorite entry form. Since it is somewhat different, I thought I'd share the pattern (pages 92–93). The pattern is for an 8" finished block, although the finished size of my blocks is 9½", dictated by the grid of the Navajo block.

For the Sunflower block, you need an 8½" x 8½" square of fabric for the background. Trace the templates for the star, flower, and flower center onto the paper side of a piece of fus-ible web of your choice. Cut out the center of each traced piece ¼" inside your drawn line. Fuse the web to the wrong side of your fabric. Cut out your shape, exactly on the drawn line. Arrange the pieces on your background and fuse, following the manufacturer's instructions. You may want to cut out the fabric behind the star and sunflower before adding the flower center, as there will be four thicknesses of fabric if you do not. Stitch around each fused piece and you're done!

Finalist
Bill and Judy Woodworth
Gering, Nebraska

Photo by Judy Woodworth

Meet Bill and Judy

Bill and I were high-school sweethearts who have lived a full life together, married for 43 years, while the last dozen years have mostly revolved around quilting. I admit I had to drag my husband into this creative, incredibly fun world of quilting because I didn't want to go on this journey alone.

He has always been my best friend and goes with me to quilt shows. He hauls all my suitcases full of quilts and class supplies. He has watched me design and go through the long process of making show quilts. He has driven me thousands of miles and kept me on schedule. He's also a very talented painter. He even dyes some of my fabrics that I use in my quilts.

My husband's full-time banking job at times has been stressful. I decided I needed to find a way to involve him in my quilting world as an outlet for relieving stress. I showed him all the quilts that were being painted and pleaded for his help. I think I finally just wore him out with my begging. To date we have made five quilts together. All he asks is that I don't make him speak at my classes, or write anything, or tell anyone that he's a quilter—well I kept most of my promises.

For those people who started quilting later in their life, I want you to know you should dream big. I only started making quilts 15 years ago, and have been a professional longarm quilter and teacher for the last 12 years. I have been fortunate enough to win many big international awards, some with my good friends Mary Sue Suit and Joan Davis.

I have my first quilting book, *Freemotion Quilting Handbook*, coming out in 2010, published by the American Quilter's Society. I've also had the fun experience of being on *The Quilt Show* with Alex Anderson and Ricky Tims. And the best dream of all is working with my husband on these painted wholecloth quilts.

Since I got started late I had a lot to learn, and techniques were changing almost from one book to the next. I tried everything and every style. I believe, at age 61, that I am only at the beginning of this journey.

Inspiration and Design

I love sunflowers so I knew I had to do this challenge. I even grew giant sunflowers this year for inspiration. They grew taller than my roof (fig. 1). Some of the pictures I took had the bricks as the backdrop and I knew I would include bricks and sunflowers in my quilt or quilting.

Fig. 1

Graffiti, Sunflowers & Bricks

71" x 71"

I started drafting distorted sunflowers looking both at my pictures and also observing a Sunflower block. I decided to cube the different sunflowers. As I thought about piecing the cubed flowers, they started looking like something I had seen in graffiti art. I looked at my husband watching a football game and a light bulb went off.

"Honey, do you think we could do a graffiti quilt? A painted graffiti quilt?" The look he gave me was—well, let's just say I let him watch his football game. But I wasn't going to give up.

After I had drawn four or five cubed sunflowers, I scanned them into my computer and started playing with them in CorelDraw® software. They really excited me. I decided to go online and look at all the graffiti artists. They were amazing. I found a Web site called The Graffiti Creator at http://www.graffiticreator.net.

You could type in a word, then stretch it, distort it, overlap in any way you could imagine, and even color it. I did two words with my own design, "Sunflower" and "Power." Then I downloaded it, and starting having more fun.

Technique

If you scan your work into a software program that turns your sketch into a vector drawing, then you can import it to CorelDraw. Each area of the sketch becomes a closed patchwork shape. At that point you can move it around, stretch it, color it, and add more design. I first learned how to do this in a Caryl Bryer Fallert class.

I was originally going to have Sunflower Power graffiti with the cubed sunflowers around it but I could not get a balanced design. After I took out the word "power," it was well balanced but lacked something. In the graffiti pictures I had seen, there were lots of lines going to an off-centered focal point (fig. 2). I drew this into my design and colored it. I liked knowing I would have room to quilt in the texture of the bricks I had envisioned.

Fig. 2

I enlarged the drawing to the size I wanted and printed using the tiling option in CorelDraw. I taped all the 8½" x 11" sheets together into a full-size master pattern of the quilt and transferred the design to the white cotton sateen. Since Bill was going to paint before I quilted, I transferred the design with black fabric markers.

I told Bill I wanted the graffiti to have a distressed look, as if the colors were painted outdoors. To keep the paint a little thicker and with more intense colors, he mixed the Setacolor paints with Aloe Vera 100% Gel instead of water. Sharon Schamber gave us this tip. It also seemed to keep the paint from bleeding into the other areas. After it dried, I ironed it completely on the front and the back of the quilt to set the color and make it permanent.

I used two battings, wool and cotton, and a cotton sateen backing. I quilted it using heavy cotton thread over the black lines. I used Superior thread in my bricks and some silk thread in my

sunflowers. I wanted the contemporary brick textures mixed with swirling cracks.

I finished the quilt with an envelope-style facing. To make the back interesting, I used Aleene's® Jewel-It® Embellishing Glue, then sprinkled it with glitter. After it dried overnight I used my vacuum cleaner attachment to remove the excess glitter. I also used Bo-Nash's foiling glue and drew a design around the black facing. This foiling glue dries overnight. Then you take the foil, colored side facing up, and press it with your fingers on the foil over the dried glue. As you can see it gives it a wonderful colored permanent design.

What a fun journey and who better to share it with than my wonderful husband!

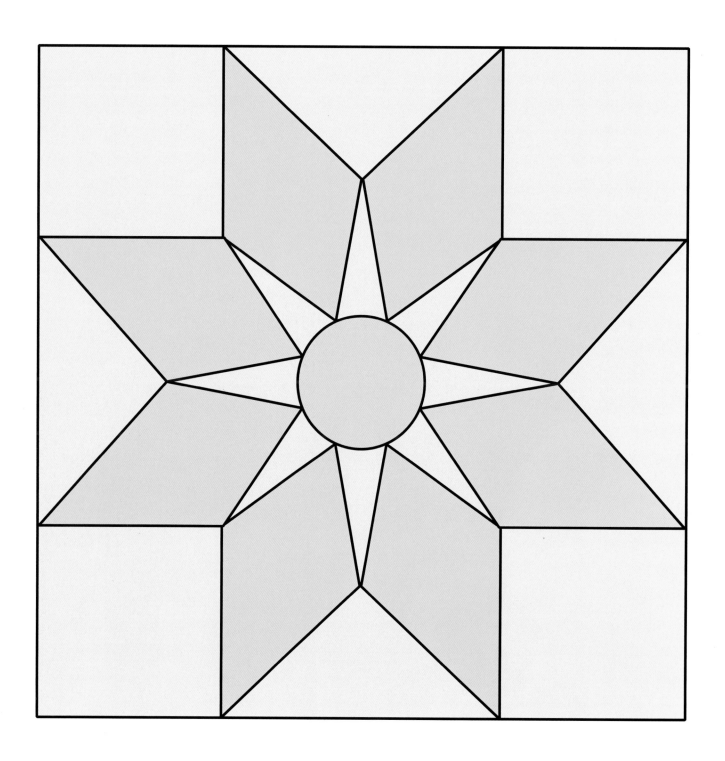

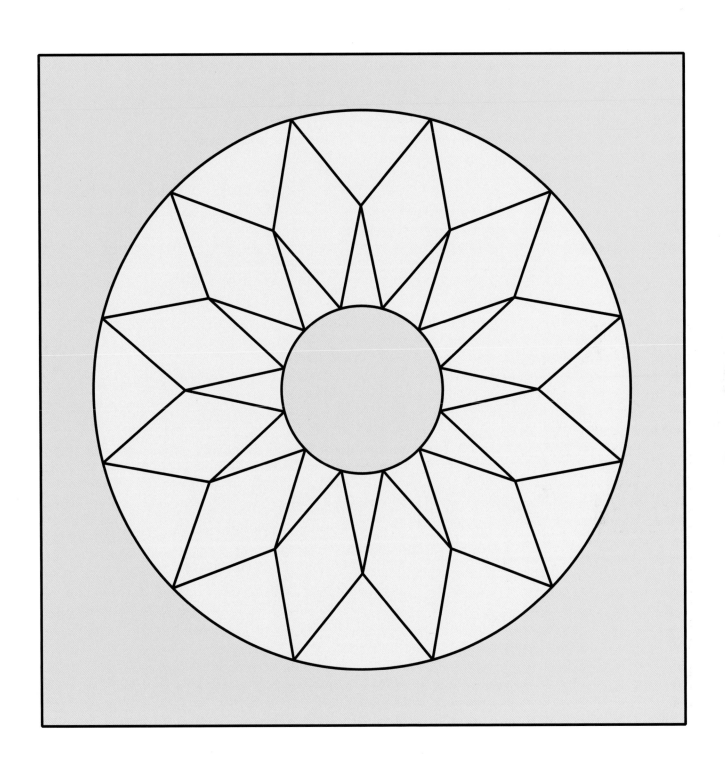

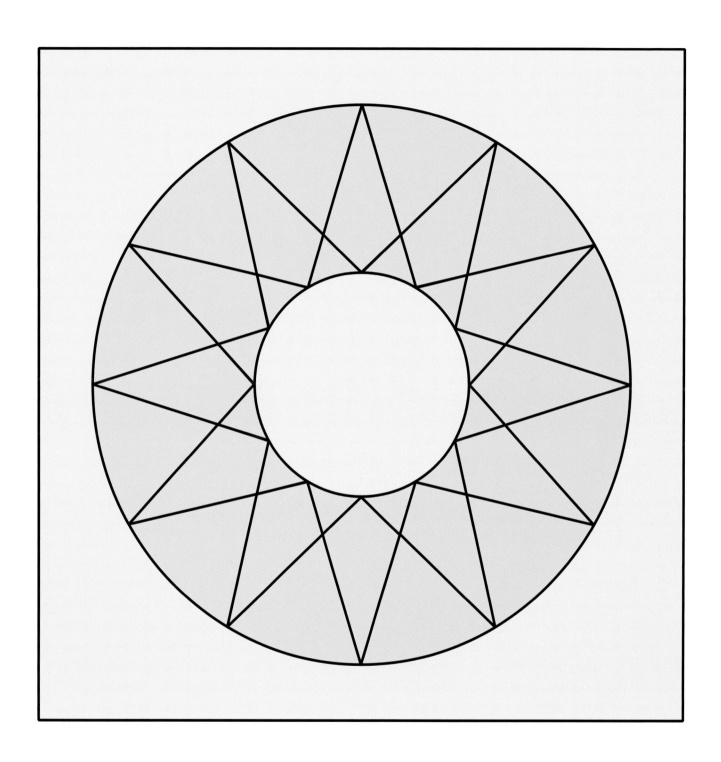

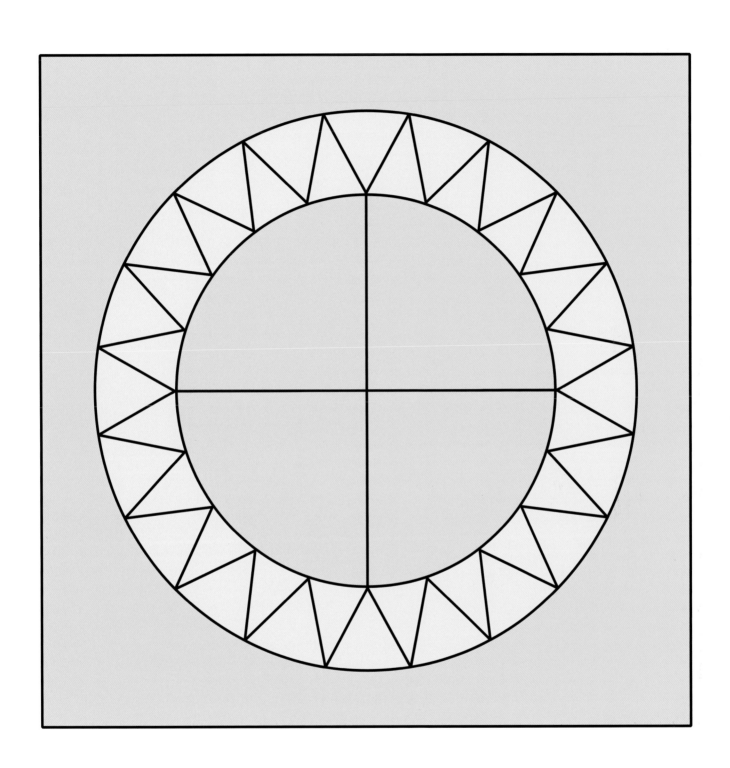

The National Quilt Museum

The National Quilt Museum is the world's largest and foremost museum devoted to quilts and the only museum dedicated to today's quilts and quiltmakers. Established in 1991 by American Quilter's Society founders Bill and Meredith Schroeder as a not-for-profit organization, the museum is located in a 27,000 square foot facility in Paducah, Kentucky. It was designed specifically to exhibit quilts aesthetically and safely. Three expansive galleries that envelop visitors in color, design, and exquisite stitchery feature ten to twelve exhibits annually.

In July 2008, the United States Congress designated the Museum of the American Quilter's Society as The National Quilt Museum of the United States. While the designation does not come with federal funding, it provides national recognition of the museum's significance and stature as a national cultural and educational treasure.

The highlight of any visit is The William & Meredith Schroeder Gallery with a rotating exhibit of quilts from the museum's collections of over 300 quilts. The nucleus of the collection is composed of extraordinary contemporary quilts collected privately by the Schroeders and donated to the museum. The collection continues to expand with the addition of purchase award quilts from the annual AQS Quilt Show & Contest and with the additions by purchase or donation of exceptional quilts selected to enhance the collection. In 2006, Oh Wow!—a stunning collection of more than 40 miniature quilts—was added to the collection.

Educational programs offered in three well-equipped classrooms serve local and national audiences. The museum offers an annual schedule of in-depth workshops taught by master quilters. Educational activities are also offered for youth including hands-on projects, summer quilt camps, a junior quilter and textile artist club, and the School Block Challenge, a national initiative. Exhibitions like New Quilts from an Old Favorite,

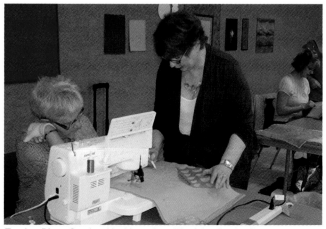

Teacher Diane Gaudynski with student. Photo by Jessica Byassee.

is truly an exhilarating place to learn more about quilts, quiltmaking, and quilters.

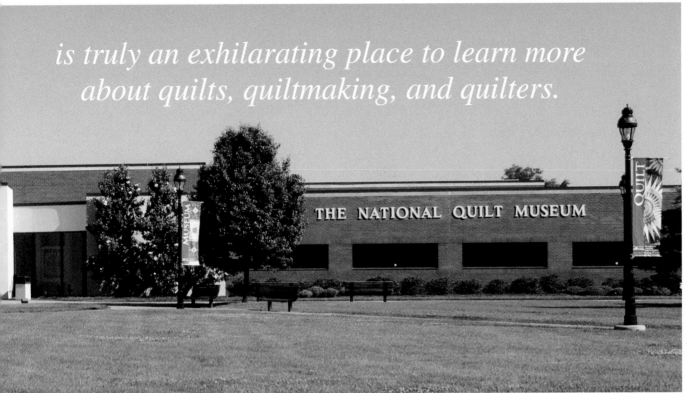

which are developed by the museum, travel to other galleries and museums across the United States, helping to educate and inspire a wider spectrum of viewers.

With more than 700 quilt-related book titles available, the museum's bookstore has one of the largest selections of quilt books anywhere. In addition, the museum's shop offers quilts and quilt-related merchandise as well as fine crafts by artisans from the region and beyond. The entire facility is wheelchair accessible.

Located at 215 Jefferson Street in historic downtown Paducah, Kentucky, the museum is open year-round 10 am to 5 pm, Monday through Saturday,

Student in Karen Kay Buckley's clas

and 1–5 on Sundays, April through October. Check the museum's Web site, www.quiltmuseum.org, for extended hours during special events. Museum programs and events can also be found on the Web site. For more information, e-mail info@quiltmuseum.org, call 270-442-8856, or write to The National Quilt Museum, PO Box 1540, Paducah, Kentucky 42002-1540.